T0254825

Lecture Notes of the Institute for Computer Sciences, Social Informatics and Telecommunications Engineering 307

More information about this series at http://www.springer.com/series/8197

Cristina Sylla · Ido Iurgel (Eds.)

Technology, Innovation, Entrepreneurship and Education

3rd EAI International Conference, TIE 2019
Braga, Portugal, October 17–18, 2019
Proceedings

 Springer

Editors
Cristina Sylla
University of Minho
Braga, Portugal

Ido Iurgel
Rhine-Waal University of Applied Sciences
Kamp-Lintfort, Nordrhein-Westfalen
Germany

ISSN 1867-8211   ISSN 1867-822X   (electronic)
Lecture Notes of the Institute for Computer Sciences, Social Informatics
and Telecommunications Engineering
ISBN 978-3-030-40179-5   ISBN 978-3-030-40180-1   (eBook)
https://doi.org/10.1007/978-3-030-40180-1

This Springer imprint is published by the registered company Springer Nature Switzerland AG
The registered company address is: Gewerbestrasse 11, 6330 Cham, Switzerland

Preface

We are delighted to introduce the proceedings of the Third European Alliance for Innovation (EAI) International Conference on Technology, Innovation, Entrepreneurship and Education (TIE 2019), held in Braga, Portugal, October 17–18, 2019. TIE provides a platform where academics and practitioners from multi and cross-disciplinary fields such as education, artistic creation, creative industries, and business come together to collaborate and network. The event encourages the exploration of synergies that arise from different perspectives, becoming a scientific forum for promoting new venture creation opportunities. In this third edition of TIE we had an acceptance rate of 30% with a total of 42 submitted and 14 accepted papers. This was a smaller conference than planned, and the gathering turned out to be exceptionally friendly and productive. Attendees meet like-minded people and easily engaged in fruitful discussions and debates.

The TIE 2019 opening keynote was given by Prof. Andrew Manches, Director of the Children and Technology group and Deputy Director of Research and Knowledge Exchange in the School of Education at the University of Edinburgh. Prof. Andrew's research focuses on the role of physical interaction in learning and its implications for emerging technologies. His passion is bridging cognitive theory with everyday practice and design. In this endeavor he works closely with a range of formal and informal practitioners to develop educational resources – from card games to physical-digital museum exhibits. Prof. Andrew is also the founder and director of the company PlayTalkLearn.

TIE 2019 took place in Braga, one of most vibrant technology hubs in Portugal. In the late 20th century, the city bore witness to a new generation of artists and entrepreneurs that transformed the local creative ecosystem by combining art with technology and innovation. Ever since, Braga hosts high profile and international tech companies and media art productions, and these are the main drivers of the local creative economy. In 2017, this dynamic led to Braga's introduction into UNESCO's prestigious Creative City of Media Arts Network (UCCN), out of a restricted selection of 116 cities from 54 countries. For Braga, media arts also provide an opportunity to engage its citizens in rethinking the city, by reinforcing linkages between art, science, technology, and sense of community.

The TIE 2019 social events created fruitful opportunities to discuss and network e.g., the gala dinner, held at Paço do Vitorino (http://www.pacodevitorino.com), a heritage hotel located in Ponte de Lima, one of the most characterful and charming towns in northern Portugal. The House, dating back to the 16th century, is a municipal monument and has been in the same family since the mid-16th century. The history of the house is marked by several events that mime and mirror the history of Portugal.

Paço do Vitorino impresses visitors with its harmonious baroque ensemble and monumental gardens, which are accredit to the famous Italian master Nicolau Nasoni.

October 2019

Cristina Sylla
Ido Iurgel

Organization

Steering Committee

Imrich Chlamtac   Bruno Kessler Professor, University of Trento, Italy

General Chairs

Cristina Sylla   University of Minho, Portugal
Ido A. Iurgel   Rhine-Waal University of Applied Sciences, Germany

Program Chairs

Teresa Romao   Universidade NOVA de Lisboa, Portugal
Tonguc Sezen   Rhine-Waal University of Applied Sciences, Germany

Poster and Work in Progress Chairs

Alejandro Catala Bolós   Centro Singular de Investigacion en Tecnoloxias da Informacion, University of Santiago de Compostela, Spain
Elena Márquez Segura   Uppsala University, Sweden

Demos Chairs

Lisa Tümmler   Ravensburger AG, Germany
Eva Brooks   Aalborg University, Denmark

Web Chairs

João Martinho Moura   Polytechnic Institute of Cávado and Ave, Portugal
Cristina Sylla   University of Minho, Portugal

Communication and Social Media Chairs

Cristina Sylla   University of Minho, Portugal
Douglas Menegazzi   Federal University of Santa Catarina, Brazil

Workshop Chairs

Digdem Sezen   Istanbul University, Turkey
Susanne Haake   Pädagogische Hochschule Weingarten, Germany

Sponsorship and Exhibits Chair

Cristina Sylla   University of Minho, Portugal

Publication Chair

Marco Zappatore   University of Salento, Italy

Local Chair

Carla Antunes   University of Minho, Portugal

Conference Manager

Kristina Lappyova   EAI

Technical Program Committee

Eduardo Dias	NOVA-LINCS, Universidade NOVA de Lisboa, Portugal
Adérito Marcos	Universidade Aberta, Portugal
Alex Mitchell	National University of Singapore, Singapore
Alejandro Catalá Bolós	University of Santiago de Compostela, Spain
Ana Paula Afonso	Universidade de Lisboa, Portugal
Ana Paula Cláudio	Universidade de Lisboa, Portugal
Annika Wolff	LUT University, Finland
Anton Nijholt	University of Twente, The Netherlands
António Coelho	FEUP, Portugal
Bruno Cardoso	KU Leuven, Belgium
Chamari Edirisinghe	Independent Researcher, Malaysia
Clara Coutinho	University of Minho, Portugal
Chrystalla Neophytou	Open University, Cyprus
Diogo Cabral	IST, Portugal
Digdem Sezen	Istanbul University, Turkey
Elena Márquez Segura	Uppsala University, Sweden
Eva Brooks	University of Aalborg, Denmark
Eva Cerezo	Universidad de Zaragoza, Spain
Eva Oliveira	Polytechnic Institute of Cávado and Ave, Portugal
Fernando Birra	Universidade NOVA de Lisboa, Portugal
Filomena Soares	University of Minho, Portugal
Frank Zimmer	Rhine-Waal University of Applied Sciences, Germany
Guenter Wallner	University of Applied Arts Vienna, Austria
Javier Marcos	Universidad de Zaragoza, Spain
José Creissac Campos	University of Minho, Portugal
Maria Beatriz Carmo	Universidade de Lisboa, Portugal
Mel Krokos	University of Portsmouth, UK

Contents

Innovating Methods

Innovating and Exploring Children's Learning

Reading to Level Up: Gamifying Reading Fluency

Diğdem Sezen[1], Ute Massler[2(✉)], Pedro Ribeiro[3], Susanne Haake[2],
Ido Iurgel[3], and Anabela Parente[3]

[1] Istanbul University, Kaptanı Derya Ibrahim Pasa sk.,
Vezneciler, 34116 Istanbul, Turkey
dsezen@istanbul.edu.tr
[2] University of Education Weingarten, Weingarten, Germany
{massler, haake}@ph-weingarten.de
[3] Rhine-Waal University of Applied Sciences, Kamp-Lintfort, Germany
{pr, ii, apr}@hsrw.eu

Abstract. Employing game design elements to create an environment for struggling readers to read accurately, with proper speed and right expression might inspire them to continue practising and help their teachers incorporate engaging tools in their instructional repertoire for fluent reading. The EU-funded innovation project GameLet aims at developing digital media-based gamification tools to enhance student motivation in self-directed, individual and cooperative learning phases for reading fluency training. A fictional audio play production is one centrepiece of the developed game concept. This paper specifically focuses on the game design ideas related to the Recording Studio, a particular part of this gamified audio play environment, and discusses minigames ideas related to this concept as strategies to improve reading fluency. These gamification ideas exemplify the plethora of available opportunities to gamify the acquisition of reading fluency.

Keywords: Reading fluency · Gamification · Educational game design

1 Introduction

Selecting and facilitating effective individual and collaborative methods and tools for fostering reading fluency is crucial for teachers to motivate student interest and attention to reading. Gamifying these tools might inspire students to continue practising and help teachers incorporate engaging tools in their instructional repertoire for training reading fluency. Game-based reading exercises might promote 'situated learning' [1] that allows deeper and more meaningful avenues to create, assess, analyse and apply new skills and knowledge.

Focusing on improving the reading skills of schoolchildren by taking a gamified media-supported approach, The European Union funded the interdisciplinary innovation project GameLet which targets "to increase struggling readers' reading fluency, to foster their multilingualism and to contribute to their media literacy based on the comprehensive integration of digital media in trainings" [2]. The overall project not

C. Sylla and I. Iurgel (Eds.): TIE 2019, LNICST 307, pp. 3–12, 2020.
https://doi.org/10.1007/978-3-030-40180-1_1

only develops gamified multilingual learning environments and materials but also focuses on developing training modules for teachers and contributing to the theoretical discussions in relation to gamification and educational media design [3]. The "meaningful" digital media-based gamification mechanisms applied in GameLet aim at enhancing pupils' motivation in self-directed, individual and cooperative learning phases for RF training. A fictional audio play production is the centrepiece of the concept designed to encourage pupils to improve their reading and successfully record their role.

This paper focuses on the Recording Studio game design ideas, a particularly important segment of the game environment, and discusses the mini-games under the Recording Studio section concerning gamification ideation techniques and strategies to improve reading fluency.

2   Reading Fluency

When reading, learners have to cope with at least two cognitive tasks - word recognition and comprehension. As LaBerge & Samuels [4] explain, the more attention readers have to pay to word recognition, the less they can give to comprehension. On the contrary, fluent readers who recognise words and sentences effortlessly have more cognitive resources available for text comprehension. They can make connections among the ideas in the text as well as between the text and their background knowledge [5]. Thus, fluency serves as a bridge between word recognition and word comprehension. It is defined by the National Reading Panel [6] as the basic reading skill which enables readers to assign word meanings reliably and quickly at the level of letters, words, sentences and text passages, in order to read aloud texts at an appropriate reading speed and to be able to intonate them in a meaning-oriented way.

Developing an appropriate reading fluency is especially important for struggling readers as they are likely to remain poor readers throughout their lives no matter how bright they are [6]. Effective methods to develop reading accuracy, fluency, as well as comprehension, require students to repeatedly read passages orally with guidance and feedback [6]. However, as effective as such programs may be, our observations indicate that student motivation to engage in these activities fades quickly due to the programs' monotony [3]. A reading fluency training method that tries to provide an authentic context for the practising of reading skills is the Readers' Theater. Here, cooperating groups of pupils train their reading fluency using dialogical texts, with the roles of speakers and narrators distributed in the groups. Finally, the practised texts are presented in a creative form in the plenum [7]. The Readers' Theater integrates repeated reading aloud sessions as the central training technique as well as providing and receiving feedback from teachers and learners. Following a bilingual or multilingual approach, the Multilingual Readers' Theater (MELT) integrates school and foreign languages as well as migration languages [8]. Thus, MELT responds to social demands on multilingualism as an expectation of competence [9] and to the individual multilingual reality of learners [8].

GameLet integrates a wide variety of reading training methods, some of which will be described in the article. It also extends the MELT approach by applying gamified learning scenarios and materials, including interactive elements and adding media-based assessment and feedback forms. The aim is to intensify reading fluency training on an individual and a cooperative basis, and to increase the extent of self-learning phases through media support services [3].

3 Gamifying Reading Fluency

In playing the GameLet - learning scenario, the students act as speakers who have been selected to produce an audio play. In doing so, they go through all the tasks needed on their mission to finish the audio play. The Recording Studio is an important part of the GameLet learning scenario. It includes all the essential elements of audio play production: listening to texts, recording, selecting or deleting versions, and then sending the recorded files to receive feedback. Two possibilities exist for recording with regard to the methodology of the Readers' Theater: single roles or synchronous group performance. The progress of the performance is documented in a leaderboard. The leaderboard shows the individual progress as well as the progress of the group. A significant challenge within the Gamelet approach is to increase the intensity of the exercise in a self-directed context. In addition, solutions are being explored to increase the motivation to practice student reading fluency with gamified units that complement the basic functions of the Recording Studio, some of which will be presented in this article.

Addressing GameLet's specific objectives directed toward self-directed and intensified learning and practice, the Recording Studio concept involves a cluster of mini-game design ideas based on repetitive use of "reading" as the primary game verb. The game verb in the context of game design describes the action executed by the player to achieve a goal in the game and this action changes the game state. Anthropy and Clark [10] refer to a game verb as the rules that allow the player to interact with the other rules in the game and create a dialogue between game and player. Recording Studio mini-games give a player only one basic action: "Read". As Jesse Schell mentioned in the Art of Game Design, "If you give a player a gun that can only shoot bad guys, you have a very simple game. But if that same gun can also be used to shoot a lock off a door, break a window, hunt for food, pop a car tire, or write messages on the wall, you now start to enter a world of many possibilities" [11]. Following this logic, in Recording Studio games, by increasing the number of things that you can do only by reading, the number of playful actions increases as well.

Reading fluency requires practice across days or weeks to internalise reading concepts and techniques. Instead of sitting down for long hours to practice reading, short game sessions, carried out multiple times a day, similar to the playing of casual mobile games, could be preferable for students to practice their reading. Employing a mobile game player interaction approach could allow students to practice for brief periods spanning across days or weeks or even months, and so internalise the techniques in the long run. With an approach emphasising the playful side of reading as a study subject, the gamification design group of the GameLet project examined the traditional classroom methods for improving reading fluency and focused on the exercises that students and teachers experienced as game-like. The preliminary design ideas for mini-games involve mediating these experiences with digitally enriched gamification elements. In that way, the design group aimed to achieve the quality of the mediated player experience without sacrificing either educational objectives or ludic attributes.

4   Let the "Freeze-Frame" Speak: Showing and Sharing Text Understanding

Reading a literary text aloud well is only possible if readers understand what they are reading, which means understanding what conflicts characters experience, what kind of relationship they have with other characters or what situations they are in. If students' understanding of the text is poor, they find it more difficult to read fluently and, in particular, to pronounce the text using appropriate emphasis. Consequently, fostering but also assessing students' understanding of the readers' theater scripts take place at the beginning of the learning process. Therefore, the freeze-frame technique might be used to focus on and clarify an essential aspect of a scene [12]. One possible way to use it within the context of the Multilingual Readers' Theater is the following: After groups have been formed, pupils read the scene assigned to their working group; first silently on their own, making sure that they comprehend what is taking place in the scene. Then, any ideas that are important to help understand the scene are discussed and clarified within the group. Now, the pupils first decide together on a situation in their scene that represents in some way something pivotal or unique (a central conflict, something comical or dramatic, etc.). This situation is then depicted by some members of the group as a single 'frozen' image. The other remaining members of the group describe the frozen scene. After the presentation of the freeze-frame in plenum, selected group members might further explain the intention of their freeze-frame if necessary. Also, a discussion to develop a deeper understanding of the presented scene can follow. Thus, the freeze-frame technique helps to work out relationships between literary figures, visualise conflicts or depict important events, thus stimulating students to actively make sense of their scene and to show their interpretations. Furthermore, the body-focused method makes it possible to empathize with a particular situation or constellation of persons, and promotes a change of perspective.

If this drama technique is transferred to a gamified and media-supported learning environment, advantages but also challenges emerge. The visualisation of the freeze-frame requires a digital version and must contend with the problem that there is no body-focused group work anymore. One solution is to implement the concept explored in the project STREEN [13] that aims the stimulation of students' reading comprehension by allowing them to collaboratively or individually author 2D illustrations (see Fig. 1). STREEN offers drag and drop mechanisms to compose an illustration by manipulating 2D graphical representations of the characters and other elements of the narrative.

The selection of objects should allow enough creative options to arrange the freeze frame, for example, the figures shown and their typical postures, or the presented objects. Further, this digital version allows the integration of recorded audio files to the collage. Essential functions of the Recording Studio, such as recording, listening and sending audio recordings, are added here and connected to the selected figures and

Fig. 1. Students creating illustrations in project STREEN [13].

objects in the freeze-frame. The finalised version of the freeze-frame can then take part in a competition with the help of peer feedback or feedback from the teacher. The freeze frame with the most votes gets the most points. Further, the digital freeze frame can be used to start a plenary discussion (Fig. 2).

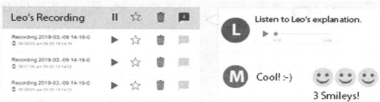

Fig. 2. Digital freeze frame.

5 Addressing Prosodic Reading as a Design Objective: "Emoji Tales" and "Maestro"

Prosody is a compilation of spoken language features that include stress or emphasis, pitch variations, intonation, reading rate, and pausing [5]. Fluent readers use prosodic or melodic features of spoken language – stress, pitch variations, intonation, rate, phrasing, and pausing – in their voices [14]. Thus, when readers embed these features in oral expression, they are giving evidence of actively interpreting or constructing meaning from the passage [14].

Regulating intonation - e.g. higher voices to express strong emotions like anger, joy or lower voices to express nonchalance or indifference - allows the reader to achieve optimal comprehension and express the emotion of the content more accurately [15]. Two mini-game concepts within GameLet, *Emoji Tales* and *Maestro*, focus on improving expressive reading skills through proper intonation and speed.

The first game, *Emoji Tales*, allows the player to read and record a text according to the adverbs suggested by the random emoji icons assigned by the game system. *Emoji Tales* employs the popular social media pictographs "emojis" as an attraction point. Emojis are ideograms used in electronic messages and web pages, and users heavily use them to colour and humanise text-based social media messages [16]. Depending on the random emojis, the student reads the text, e.g. "sadly", "happily", "angrily", "surprised", "nervously". In addition to the turn-based mimicking of different emotions, another fun factor of the game comes from the contrast of the text's content and the assigned emotion by the emoji. For example, the student might read a passage based on a love serenade angrily or a violent scene kindly and mildly.

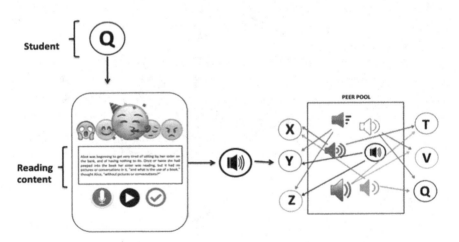

Fig. 3. The feedback cycle of the mini-game *Emoji Tales*.

The main challenge of the game is to read the passage with proper intonation, pace and emotion as the emojis change throughout the game session. When the students have completed the reading/recording mission, the mini-game allows them to listen to the recording. If they are happy with the result, they can submit the recording to the peer pool (see Fig. 3). The peer pool describes the virtual space where the students' audio clips are collected to be peer-reviewed by other students based on the strengths and weaknesses of the reading performance. How to provide feedback that is content- and style-appropriate is discussed and practised before using criteria-based feedback forms.

Submitted audio clips to the peer pool are assigned by the system to the peer students proportionately to be evaluated. With the help of the criteria-based feedback form, each student gives feedback from one star to five stars to the randomly assigned recordings of their peers. Based on the evaluations, the ones with the higher scores go up on the leaderboard. The leaderboard provides a means to reward the best readers and increase the game's replayability by allowing student players to compete. Moreover, students could also play the game in free-time mode to practice their reading. Also, teachers could choose the reading materials in the game based on their syllabi.

The second mini-game addressing the expressive reading as a design objective is the pacing game *Maestro*. In this mini-game, a student reads the text aloud and the arrows on the screen act as a conductor. "Arrow up" on the screen instructs the student to read aloud, while "arrow down" means reading aloud softly. Similarly, "arrow left" instructs the student to read fast, while the "arrow right" means to read slowly. Multiple arrows together on the screen conduct a choral reading of the selected text. The choral reading could be used for in-class collaborative live game sessions. Similar to the process of *Emoji Tales*, the students read and record their performances as an audio clip. If they are pleased with the result, they submit the clip to the peer pool to be evaluated. Each student gives feedback from one star to five stars to the randomly assigned recordings of their peers. Based on the evaluations, the ones with the higher scores go up on the leaderboards. Again, similar to the feedback cycle of *Emoji Tales*, students could also play *Maestro* in free-time mode to practice their reading and teachers have control over the selection of reading materials in the game by posting to the system.

6 Choral Reading as Collaborative Gameplay: Oratorio Dicer

Choral reading refers to the interpretive reading of the text by a group of voices. Students might read the lines, stanzas, paragraphs on their own, in pairs, or unison. Educators list numerous benefits of utilising choral reading for reading fluency. These benefits vary from improved diction to self-confidence, from increased fluency to expanded vocabulary and enjoyment of reading. Choral reading also makes the students in the classroom active participants and facilitates better comprehension of the text being read [17].

Addressing the choral reading as a design objective, the mini-game *Oratorio Dicer* aims to create a gamified "reading together" experience for the students in groups, and allows students to develop effective and fluent read-aloud skills. In the game, the system assigns a number to every student logged in to the game app. The system also randomly assigns numbers to the parts of the uploaded text (sentences, words, stanzas or paragraphs). The game system randomly throws the numbers of the text parts and the student with the matching number starts to read aloud the part by pushing the record button while reading, similar to pushing the record button when creating Instagram or Snapchat stories. The system highlights her/his part in the text. While the student finishes reading the assigned part, s/he removes her/his finger from the recording button, and the student/s whose number(s) come up next continues with the reading. This game is designed to be played as part of classroom activities and requires students to follow and listen to the prior readers carefully, while maintaining their concentration on the reading material. To be successful in the game, students have to move along smoothly by reading aloud and following along with the reading of the previous reader from one sentence, line, stanza or paragraph to the next. Each reading performance must be articulated expressively and with the proper emphasis. If the pursuing reader loses track of what is being read, the system assigns another number and the assigned student keeps reading from where the prior reader left off. If losing track while reading more than three times, the student fails the game. If s/he keeps up until the end of the selected text by reading her/his parts, s/he gets points (Fig. 4).

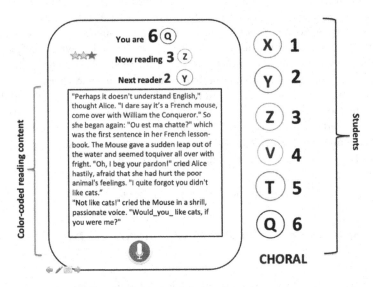

Fig. 4. *Oratorio Dicer* interface elements.

7 Gamifying Speed-Reading and Accuracy: "Speedy Reader" and "Singing in the Read"

Even though reading speed without comprehending text content is pointless, slow reading is a more severe "weakness independent of the purpose of reading" and a serious problem for learners [18]. Speed has a considerable impact on students' reading fluency. To increase their reading speed, the students need to be able to recognize and decode words with ease [19]. Improving reading speed requires timed practice. The mini-games *Speedy Reader* and *Singing in the Read* aim to stimulate not only curiosity and interest on the gamification features but also practice itself.

The first mini-game idea promoting reading speed through gamification is *Speedy Reader*. It allows students to compete to see who can read a text fastest, without any mistakes, while also comprehending the content. The students read and record the selected text as fast as they can without mistakes, and respond to the short multiple-choice test questions testing their comprehension of the text content. These multiple-choice questions are prepared and uploaded by the teacher. The students submit their audio clip to the peer pool and the game system automatically calculates their submitted test results. Based on the correct answers, the system calculates the percentage of the student's comprehension of the text. Once learners have played the game for the first time, the teacher should reflect with them on how reading speed, number of errors and text comprehension are related, as high reading speed can lead to more errors and less understanding. In addition to the test score, peer students evaluate each other's reading performances and submit their assessment based on a scale of one to five stars. The game system combines the evaluation of the test results with the peer evaluations and establishes the resulting position in the leaderboard of the game.

The second game addressing speed-reading is *Singing in the Read*. In this game, the students sing the reading text assigned by the game system to a well-known melody while trying to fit the words to the music. The game requires the readers to quickly read and grasp the words, and fit them into the melody accordingly. After having practised a few times, the player students record the reading passage with the melody, listen to the recording, and if they are satisfied with the result, submit the recording as an audio clip to the peer pool. The peer students, similar in the cycles of the previous games, review the audio recordings by allotting stars from 1 to 5. The leaderboard is ordered based on the peer-reviews.

8 Conclusion

Developing an educational game that balances both learning objectives and ludic qualities demands an understanding of both domains. The initial motivation for the ideation of the Recording Studio games involves easy access to a playful mode providing equal participation for all students. Improving reading fluency requires individual and collaborative practice, spanning time and locations (e.g. home, classroom, after school). The mini-games presented here can be used both as part of the GameLet concept as well as independently of it. The rapid idea generation for the Recording Studio, which is a sub-concept in the large-scale GameLet project, is based on the use of "reading" as the primary and only game verb to keep the focus of the game on reading practice. In other words, the winning conditions of the games are determined through the players' use of their reading skills.

The ideation process of Recording Studio games defines an initial phase of the iterative game design process. Following the preliminary process, the games will be playtested by expert groups in terms of gameplay and teaching/learning objectives. For future work, a scheduled design-thinking workshop to refine the gameplay features and improve the quality and gameplay functionality of game design is being planned. The iterative process itself will be used within a design-based research framework as successive versions of the games are implemented.

References

1. Gee, J.P.: What Video Games have to teach us about learning and literacy. Comput. Entertain. **1**, 20 (2003). https://doi.org/10.1145/950566.950595
2. Gamelet web page, https://www.gamelet.eu/. Accessed 01 Sept 2019
3. Massler, U., Gantikow, A., Haake, S., Müller, W., Lopes, C., Neofytou, C.: GameLet – fostering oral reading fluency with a gamified, media-based approach. In: 13th European Conference on Games Based Learning, Odense (2019, in press)
4. LaBerge, D., Samuels, S.J.: Toward a theory of automatic information processing in reading. Cogn. Psychol. **6**, 293–323 (1974). https://doi.org/10.1016/0010-0285(74)90015-2
5. Osborn, J., Lehr, F.: A focus on fluency. Research-based practices in early reading series. Pacific Resources for Education and Learning (PREL), Honolulu (2003)
6. National Institute of Child Health and Human Development: Report of the National Reading Panel: Teaching children to read – an evidence-based assessment of the scientific research literature on reading and its implications for reading instruction. U.S. Government Printing Office, Washington, DC (2000)
7. Mraz, M., Nichols, W., Caldwell, S., Beisley, R., Sargent, S., Rupley, W.: Improving oral reading fluency through readers theatre. Reading Horiz.: J. Literacy and Lang. Arts, **52**, 163–180 (2013)
8. Kutzelmann, S., Massler, U., Klaus, P., Götz, K., Ilg, A.: Mehrsprachiges Lesetheater: Handbuch zu Theorie und Praxis. Verlag Barbara Budrich, Leverkusen/Opladen (2017)
9. Beacco, J.-C., Byram, M.: From Linguistic Diversity to Plurilingual Education: Guide for the Development of Language Education Policies in Europe. Council of Europe, Strasbourg (2007)
10. Anthropy, A., Clark, N.: A Game Design Vocabulary: Exploring the Foundational Principles Behind Good Game Design. Addison-Wesley Professional, Boston (2014)
11. Schell, J.: The Art of Game Design: A Book of Lenses. Morgan Kaufmann Publishers Inc., San Francisco (2008)
12. Cremin, T., McDonald, R., Longley, E., Blakemore, L.: Jumpstart! Drama: Games and Activities for Ages 5–11. Routledge, Abingdon (2018)
13. Ribeiro, P., Michel, A., Iurgel, I., Ressel, C., Sylla, C., Müller, W.: Empowering children to author digital media effects for reader's theatre. In: Proceedings of the 17th ACM Conference on Interaction Design and Children, pp. 569–574. ACM, New York, (2018). https://doi.org/10.1145/3202185.3210793
14. Rasinski, T.: Assessing reading fluency. Pacific Resources for Education and Learning (PREL) (2004)
15. Rasinski, T.: Reading fluency instruction: moving beyond accuracy, automaticity, and prosody. Reading Teacher **59**, 704–706 (2011). https://doi.org/10.1598/RT.59.7.10
16. Hakami, S.: The Importance of Understanding Emoji: An Investigative Study Fax Email Print – PDFfiller (2017). http://www.cs.bham.ac.uk/~rjh/courses/ResearchTopicsInHCI/2016-17
17. McCauley, J.K., McCauley, D.S.: Using choral reading to promote language learning for ESL students. Reading Teacher **45**, 526–533 (1992)
18. Brown, P.J., Hirst, S.B.: Writing reading courses: the interrelationship of theory and practice. In: Language Teaching Projects for the Third World. ELT Documents 116. Pergamon Press, Oxford (1983)
19. Jenkins, J.R., Fuchs, L.S., van den Broek, P., Espin, C., Deno, S.L.: Sources of individual differences in reading comprehension and reading fluency. J. Educ. Psychol. **95**, 719–729 (2003). https://doi.org/10.1037/0022-0663.95.4.719

Rethinking the Design of Hotspots in Children's Digital Picturebooks: Insights from an Exploratory Study

Douglas Menegazzi[1(✉)], Cristina Sylla[2], and Stephania Padovani[3]

[1] Federal University of Santa Catarina, Florianópolis, Brazil
douglas.menegazzi@ufsc.br
[2] University of Minho, Braga, Portugal
cristina.sylla@ie.uminho.pt
[3] Federal Univeristy of Paraná, Curitiba, Brazil
stephania.padovani@gmail.com

Abstract. Finding the correct hotspots when interacting with digital picturebooks is oft challenging for children. Here, we present an exploratory study carried out with a group of third graders to inform the design of hotspot icons for a children's digital picturebook. Based on a selection and analysis of the most commonly used icons in digital picturebooks, especially apps, we created a low fidelity paper prototype to investigate children's preferences and understanding of the interactive navigation areas, configuration and menus. For this, we invited the children to draw new icons for each hotspot. Based on the analysis of the results we designed a proposal of icons that were implemented in a digital prototype for tablets. The prototype was then validated with a similar group of children, and the results provided valuable insights for the design of hotspots that can be useful for researchers and designers working and developing digital picturebooks for children.

Keywords: Interaction design · User-centered design · Children's book apps

1 Introduction

The ability to read and process multimedia texts is a fundamental skill, with an increasing number of readers becoming familiar with convergent interactive multimedia products [1]. Technologies that were originally unrelated are increasingly becoming integrated and unified as they develop and advance. "Today, digital picturebooks are often the first literature young children engage with" [2:1]. In this context, the use of digital picturebooks during childhood provides a good opportunity to develop these skills contributing to influence reading frequency [2, 3].

However, along with the opportunities provided by the wide variety of new educational platforms and interactive mobile devices parents and researchers have also raised concerns about the drawbacks that these new technologies may pose for the socio-cognitive development of young children [4]. There is also a lack of publishing standards and an absence of design guidelines for the design of children's digital picturebooks, and apps in particular [5]. The present criticism on children's digital

C. Sylla and I. Iurgel (Eds.): TIE 2019, LNICST 307, pp. 13–22, 2020.
https://doi.org/10.1007/978-3-030-40180-1_2

books refers mainly to the often indiscriminate and poor design of multimedia and interaction resources [2, 6]. The integration of the latter needs to be well planned in order to engage the readers, keeping their attention focused on the digital picturebook, contributing to the story or to the task at hand while avoiding interrupting the narrative flow or distracting the users [7].

The interaction areas in children's digital picturebooks, also called hotspots, are usually highlighted as problematic [8]. When poorly designed, when too much or accidentally incorporated into the digital picturebook, they provide unnecessary stimuli [3] that can lead to impaired learning [5], undermining the understanding of the story [7, 8], distracting and compromising the reading experience.

Prior work has investigated, how six-to-eight-years old children – the period where children acquire literacy skills – accompanied by reading mediators interact with children's story apps [9]. The study concluded that very often neither the children nor their parents were able to identify and to find the icon buttons of the interactive areas in the app and that one of the main interaction problems with story apps was the graphic design of the hotspots.

Building on this work, our research investigates aspects related to the design of hotspots in children's picturebook apps, namely: (a) icon's content, (b) visual representation of the icons, (c) location on the book pages and on the screen. We focus on navigation hotspots, menus, and configuration areas of the app. Here, we present an intervention aimed at identifying children's needs and preferences for these hotspots.

2 Function and Affordances of Hotspots in Children's Digital Picturebooks

In the early electronic books, which run on computers, the "hotspots" originally indicated the areas on which the readers needed to click to activate sounds, animations, videos and other features, or to navigate thought the digital book [10]. Nowadays, in a scenario where mobile interactive devices are popular, hotspots are understood as "specific areas on the screen where readers can touch, slide or squeeze the surface of the device to generate sounds, animations or even content during reading" [11: 510].

Hotspots in children's picturebook apps are linked to several modalities such as sonorous, visual and haptic, among others [12]. The quality of children's digital books depends largely on the interdependence of resources to create a unified literary experience [13]. The design and integration of hotspots needs to be careful considered to provide a multimedia convergence and appropriate interaction for the readers. In order to use the hotspots, the users need to understand their affordances [14]. Particularly for children it is important to adequate the graphic, verbal and iconic representations to their level of comprehension [5, 13] to benefit from a digital picturebook.

The design of hotspots in children's picturebook apps should guide the reader through verbal, pictorial or iconic instructions in a way that does not disturb reading, but instead integrating interactive features into the narrative [15]. Therefore, a design that promotes a deeper immersion while still being congruent with the story has the potential to stimulate high levels of engagement and reading comprehension through interactive digital books [7]. In this sense, what may appear to be minor modifications in the design of hotspots may significantly improve the readers' experience and the potential of children's picturebook apps [16].

A recent study showed that there are at least 13 different kinds of hotspots according to their respective functions [15]. Among them are game hotspots, control of video and animations, hotspots of virtual or augmented reality interaction, and personalization of the book interface or the reading mode. Here, we focus on three types of hotspots [15] usually presented as buttons: (1) navigation hotspots, which are essential for the reader to access different areas of the book and turn the pages; (2) menu hotspots, which provide access to a list of options, e.g., book chapters; and (3) configuration hotspots, which allow the readers to configure the settings, such as sound and automatic reading.

3 Exploratory Study

Given the importance of involving children in the design of technology [17], which can strongly contribute to improve its quality by providing designers a better understanding of their needs [17, 18], we carried out an exploratory study with a group of children using a low fidelity paper prototype. The study aimed at assessing children's preferences for hotspots icons and understanding how to design them in accordance to children's interests. In the following sections we describe the intervention.

3.1 Participants

The study took place at a public primary school's library and it was carried out with a group of nine third graders ages eight and nine. The investigation was agreed with the school principal and the teacher, who had previously requested the parents' consent for their children to participate in the study. All the children were familiar with tablets, smartphones and digital books. The majority of them had access to tablet devices and internet at home and at least seven of them had already read book apps.

3.2 Study Design

Prior to the study, we carefully identified the most commonly used hotspot icons in a sample of ten commercial book apps for children, and choose for each hotspot the three icons that appeared most frequently. We printed each selected icon on a small paper card (5 cm × 5 cm) (see Fig. 1) and created a paper prototype that simulated two pages of a children's book app. One page represented the home page and the other represented an inner page. Additionally, we invited the children to draw their own version of the hotspots.

Fig. 1. The researcher observing the children choosing their preferred icon cards for the hotspots "start reading" (left) and "navigation to the home page" (right).

3.3 Procedure and Data Collection

One child at a time - chosen randomly by the teacher - come to the library. The paper prototype, and a set of color pencils were displayed on the table where the child and the researcher sat. A smartphone placed on a tripod with a fixed focus on children's hand movements recorded their interactions. The researcher started by presenting himself to the child and then explained the procedure. Next, he collected children' demographic data, such as use of mobile devices, internet use, familiarity with digital picture books. The same protocol was followed with every child. The study lasted about 30 min per child and comprised three assessment phases: (i) children's preferred icons, (ii) their preferences for the location of the hotspots, (iii) children's visual preferences of the hotspots. The data was collected through observation, field notes, photographs, drawings made by the children and video recordings. In the following we describe the assessment phases.

3.3.1 Assessing Children's Preferred Icons

In order to identify if the child knew the function of the hotpot icons represented on the paper cards, the researcher used the paper prototype representing the app and the paper cards representing the ten hotspots and asked the children to use them. For this he showed one representation of each hotspot (three cards). Then he displayed all the three representations for each hotspot and asked the children to order them according to their function (see Fig. 1). After that the researcher asked the children to choose a preferred representation for each function. Figure 2 (first row) displays children's most preferred items chosen from the ten hotspots selected for the survey. Children's preference for specific icons show their familiarity with other digital products, e.g., *YouTube*. For instance, the gear icon (f) is often used in games or for changing the language and other user settings. One of the microphone representations (i) for "recording reading" was significantly preferred over other and our hypotheses is that this is because the first one is an icon widely used in communication/message apps used by children.

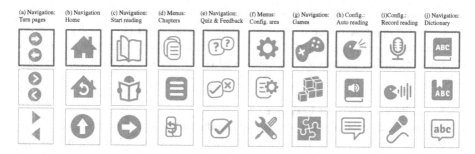

Fig. 2. The 3 different proposals for each hotspot where the first row displays children's preferred choices.

3.3.2   Children's Positioning of Hotspots

Following the first assessment, the researcher invited the children to position their preferred hotspot icon card on the picturebook app prototype. The researcher ensured that the child remembered the function of each hotspot and, if necessary, he explained the purpose of each button (see Fig. 3).

Fig. 3. Child observing the paper prototype with chosen hotspot cards, the home page (left) and an inner page (right).

From the interaction layouts created by the children we observed that they usually positioned the hotspot icons as buttons on the edges of the pages, and rarely on the inside area. An exception was the navigation hotspot (arrows), which some children positioned horizontally, on the middle of the pages.

Regarding the "home" representation, the children positioned similar hotspots together according to their function and icon appearance. For example, in most cases they placed the hotspots for the "games" and for the "quiz" side by side. The "microphone" icon (used to record reading) was placed close to the "speech" icon (used to hear a narrated version of the story). In general, in the inner app pages the "home" hotspot was positioned on the top left-hand corner of the paper prototype, whereas, the "configuration" and the "menu" hotspots (to access different pages and chapters) were placed on the opposite bottom side, near the edge of the paper (see Fig. 3).

The positioning of the hotspot icons by the children shows that they are used to manipulating digital devices and are influenced by the layout of games *and YouTube* videos.

3.3.3   Children's Hotspot Creation

In the third stage of the intervention, we invited the children to draw icons for each of the hotspots (see Fig. 4). We made clear that they were free to reproduce an icon that they liked and that represented a certain interaction, or instead to create new icons, that could better represent the activity linked to it. We observed that the task was easy for most of the children, but they had some difficulties, specially to represent the "configuration" icon (f). To represent this icon the children did not create any innovative drawings, they just copied in their own way one of the options that we had previously showed them. Our hypothesis is that this is because this specific icon groups a menu for choosing different user settings (select language, enable/disable automatic reading and sounds), being a more complex representation if compared to other hotspots. Most of the drawings are re-readings of the previously chosen icons (see Fig. 2), however, interesting new ideas have also emerged in the intervention.

Looking at the illustrations of the ten groups of icons (see Fig. 4 - bottom), from a design and visual communication perspective [19, 20], we observed that the most expressive graphic elements on these are: (a) two-dimensionality; (b) simplification of shapes and colors; (c) line structures; (d) organic graphic style. This predominantly visual style follows the principle of graphic simplicity of shapes and colors commonly found in the current language of computer icons, flat and not skeuomorph.

Only few children filled the inner area of the drawings, so the line is the main element that creates the structure of the icons. Also, only very few children wrote text near the hotspot, showing a preference for a predominantly iconographic, nonverbal language. The graphic style that prevailed is organic, even the geometric shapes when drawn are a little curved and the strokes are tremulous, which is an expected characteristic in children's drawings.

Regarding the symbolic content of the icons, few of them are innovative when compared to the paper cards that the children used. This means that the previous proposals were well accepted and incorporated by the children in their creations. However, it is important to highlight some creative solutions draw by the children. To represent the "start reading" hotspot, one of the children represented the perspective of the reader holding the book, as opposed to the hotspot printed on the cards. For a representation of the "automatic reading" hotspot – which enables automatic reading by the device – one child drew one ear while the others drew microphones or the icon of a person talking. A child redesigned the symbol for the "quiz" and the "feedback" hotspot by replacing one of the question marks with the exclamation mark (see the red highlighted icons in Fig. 4).

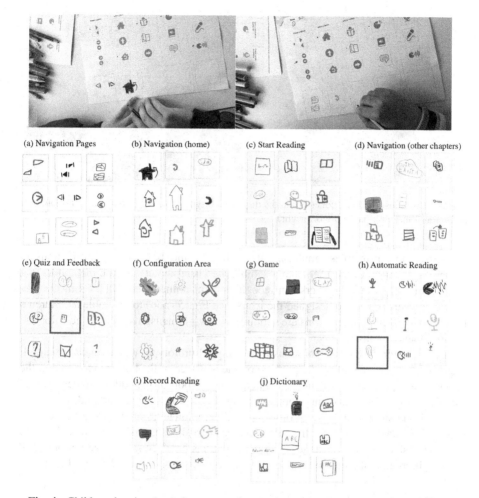

Fig. 4. Children drawing (top) the ten new hotspot icons (bottom). (Color figure online)

4 Design of Hotspot Icons for a Children's Digital Picturebook

Outgoing from the data collected in the intervention we developed a digital prototype, which contained the home page and four pages of the picturebook. To better design the new icons, we analyzed and compared all the collected data following three principles for designing graphical interfaces for children [21]: Obvious visibility; Visual resemblance; and Conceptual resemblance.

Fig. 5. The redesigned hotspots (top) in the digital prototype on the app home page (bottom left) and on an inner app page (bottom right).

These three principles emphasize that icons should be visually conspicuous to attract the attention of the users and resemble the visual features of the metaphors that they represent, so that the users can recognize them immediately [21]. From the predominant visual style, we designed the icons (see Fig. 5 - top) to resemble a children's drawing with a crayon. All icons are simplified in two-dimensions, in just one color and without internal filling.

In the design of the hotspot icons for the digital prototype, we diverged from children's preferences regarding the position on the interface of the hotspot icon to turn the pages. Instead, we positioned the pages navigation hotspots on the bottom of the page (see Fig. 5 - bottom). Besides being more convenient to use when the reader holds the digital device, this position avoids compromising the illustration areas on the inner pages, since these will contain hotspots for triggering characters and scenarios' animations. We also considered size and ideal distances recommendations between interactive buttons [21], keeping in mind that children users have less motor control of fine gestures [14].

4.1 Validation Session

A second research session was conducted in the school's library with a similar group of nine third graders ages eight and nine, to validate the icons designed in a digital prototype. The sessions lasted between 10 and 15 min per child. The children were invited to read the app on their own (without researcher intervention), and then to perform a set of tasks: (i) start the reading, (ii) navigate between pages and (iii) between chapters, (iv) change the language settings) enable/disable auto reading, (vi) return to the home page, (vii) access games, quiz and dictionary, and (viii) simulate a audio recording of reading. Each task was linked to one of the redesigned hotspots. In general, the children were able to complete all the tasks.

Besides verifying that the majority of the children were able to locate and identify the hotspot icons without problems, we noticed that they followed different paths to accomplish the same tasks. For instance, some children wanted that each page of the book contained at least the essential hotspots to navigate between pages, to reconfigure reading modes and to access the most important menus, namely: "chapters" and "home page". This indicated the need of integrating specific hotspots on pages which initially were not designed to include them.

5 Results and Conclusion

In order to design digital books for children, it is important to know children's preferences and interests. This intervention showed that children's preferences for the hotspots are tightly linked to their familiarity and use of other digital products, namely: *YouTube*, games, *Whatsapp* or other virtual messenger systems.

By involving children in the design process we received valuable insights for the design of hotspots in children's book apps. Further, a co-creation design process with children can also provide unexpected and creative graphic solutions, e.g. the "start reading" hotspot using the reader's perspective, the "automatic reading" hotspot as an ear, or the microphone hotspot as a "person talking". Or, the "quiz" and the "feedback" hotspot with an exclamation mark (see the red highlighted icons in Fig. 4).

The children also provided a simplified solution for the app navigation, choosing shorter ways to perform tasks by including essential hotspots on the book pages that were not previously included. This is, they placed the most used hotspots (to turn pages) in the internal pages close to the illustration areas of the story, which provided an efficient reading flow between pages avoiding interference with other hotspots. Children's attractive and playful drawings of the hotspot icons inspired the design of the hotspot icons for the final digital prototype. They favored a predominantly iconographic, nonverbal language, and their drawings of the hotspots showed a preference for the outline leaving the inner area empty. This demonstrates their preference for simple and "clean" icons. However, this may be related to the available materials: colored pencils, markers and crayons. Children's ideas and insights may as well be of value to researchers and designers working in the design of hotspots for children's digital picturebooks.

Acknowledgments. We thank the children from the school EB1 Gualtar, in Braga, Portugal, for their valuable contributions to this study and their teachers for allowing us to conduct this study. The first author acknowledges the fellowship from the National Council of Scientific and Technological Development – CNPq Brazil, process n: 206788/2017-7. This study has been financed by the Portuguese Foundation for Science and Technology - FCT, and European Regional Development Funds through the Competitiveness and Internationalization Operational Program reference Mobeybou-POCI-01-0145-FEDER-032580.

References

1. Ramos, G.: Habitar a infância: como ler literatura infantil. Tema Editorial, Brasília (2017)
2. Al-Yaqout, G., Nikolajva, M.: Re-conceptualising picturebook theory in the digital age. Barnelitterært Forskningstidsskrift: Nord. J. ChildLit Aesthet. **6**(1), 26971 (2015)
3. Schugar, H.R., Smith, C.A., Schugar, J.T.: Teaching with interactive picture e-books in grades K-6. Read. Teach. **66**(8), 615–624 (2013)
4. Kucirkova, N.: Digitalised early years - where next? Psychologist **24**(12), 938–940 (2011)

5. Bus, A.G., Takacs, Z.K., Kegel, C.A.T.: Affordances and limitations of electronic storybooks for young children's emergent literacy. Dev. Rev. **35**, 79–97 (2015)
6. Smeets, D.J.H., Bus, A.G.: The interactive animated e-book as a word learning device for kindergartners. Appl. Psycholinguist. **36**(4), 1–22 (2012)
7. Kao, G.Y.-M., Tsai, C.-C., Liu, C.-Y., Yang, C.-H.: The effects of high/low interactive electronic storybooks on elementary school students' reading motivation, story comprehension and chromatics concepts. Comput. Educ. **100**, 56–70 (2016)
8. Morgan, H.: Multimodal children's e-books help young learners in reading. Early Child. Educ. J. **41**(6), 477–483 (2013)
9. Menegazzi, D., Sylla, C., Padovani, S.: Hotspots in picture books apps: an investigation of the perception of readers from interaction research. In: Conference Synergy and Contradiction – How Picturebooks and Picture Books Work, pp. 39–41, University of Cambridge, Cambridge (2018)
10. Shamir, A., Korat, O.: How to select CD-ROM for young children: the teacher's role. Read. Teach. **59**, 532–543 (2006)
11. Serafini, F., Kachorsky, D., Aguilera, E.: Picture books in the digital age. Read. Teach. **69** (5), 509–512 (2016)
12. Menegazzi, D.: O Design de interfaces de livros infantis apps: uma revisão das características e recomendações. Textura **20**(43), 215–239 (2018)
13. Cahill, M., Mcgill-Frazen, A.: Selecting "app"ealing and "app"ropriate book apps for beginning readers. Read. Teach. **67**, 30–39 (2013)
14. Kamysz, K., Wichrowski, M.: A Little Goat Builds the World – An Interactive Children Story for Tablets. In: Mitchell, A., Fernández-Vara, C., Thue, D. (eds.) ICIDS 2014. LNCS, vol. 8832, pp. 228–231. Springer, Cham (2014). https://doi.org/10.1007/978-3-319-12337-0_27
15. Menegazzi, D., Sylla, C., Padovani, S.: Hotspots em livros infantis digitais: um estudo de classificação das funções. In: Proceedings of 2nd International Conference on Design and Digital Communication, pp. 45–56. IPCA, Barcelos (2018)
16. Yokota, J., Teale, W.H.: Picture books and the digital world. Read. Teach. **67**(8), 577–585 (2014)
17. Druin, A.: The role of children in the design of new technology. Behav. Inf. Technol. **21**(1), 1–25 (2002)
18. Chiu, S., Koong, C.-S., Fan, S.-H.: Icon design principles for preschoolers, implications derived from child development. Procedia – Soc. Behav. Sci. **64**, 228–237 (2015)
19. Dondis, A.D.: Sintaxe da linguagem visual, 3rd edn. Martins Fontes, São Paulo (2007)
20. Munari, B.: Design e comunicação visual. Martins Fontes, São Paulo (2001)
21. Sun, X., Plocher, T., Qu, W.: An empirical study on the smallest comfortable button/icon size on touch screen. In: Aykin, N. (ed.) UI-HCII 2007. LNCS, vol. 4559, pp. 615–621. Springer, Heidelberg (2007). https://doi.org/10.1007/978-3-540-73287-7_71

Children's Tinkering Activity with Collapse Informatics: The Internalization of Environmental Consciousness

Silvia Torsi[1,2](✉), Loredana Verardi[2], and Carmelo Ardito[2]

[1] University of Trento, via Sommarive 5 Povo, Trento, Italy
silvia.torsi@unitn.it
[2] University of Bari, via Orabona 4, Bari, Italy

Abstract. In the present paper we introduce an activity involving twenty elementary school children aimed at increasing their awareness towards the importance of reusing waste materials. Once that target is achieved, we facilitate children's purposeful construction of diegetic artefacts and imaginary robots that have environmental purposes. The main goal of the activity is to engage children in tasks through which they begin to reflect on their own future and in particular on how the current choices of the adults can influence the future of their world. The principles of collapse informatics and research through design are the basic key concepts of this project.

Keywords: Tinkering · Collapse informatics · Freire · Constructivism · Research through design

1 Introduction

What kind of world are we leaving to future generations? How does our present behaviour affect their future? Reflecting on the possible scenarios triggered by our legacy has been a recurring topic in the field of HCI (e.g. [15]). In particular, the theoretical thread of collapse informatics (e.g. [25, 26]), which draws inspiration from Jared Diamond's historical analysis what we know about of ancient societies and tries to explain their actions that led to their disappearance; massive deforestation, over-exploitation of the natural resources, soil erosion, or overpopulation are among the most relevant hypotheses [9]. In HCI, worries, anxieties and (uncomfortable) dreams have already been dealt with by Research Through Design [28], where the creation of artefacts represents the embodiment of thoughts, concepts, and constructions of prototypes, in order to foster reflection, discussion and sharing. Using dysfunctional, unpleasant, or ambiguous objects, critical design [10] aims to materialize our fear about the future. Critical objects reverberate in our minds through fascination and repulsiveness and stimulate contemplation, analysis and dialogue [11, 12]. For this activity, we found inspiration in the work of the Russian photographer Archipov [2], who describes the crisis of the post-soviet Russia through do-it-yourself (DIY) objects, and the way (impoverished) people creatively solved their daily shortages by assembling waste into useful, new objects. For the analysis part of the activity, we employed the

C. Sylla and I. Iurgel (Eds.): TIE 2019, LNICST 307, pp. 23–33, 2020.
https://doi.org/10.1007/978-3-030-40180-1_3

constructivist theory [17, 19] and the process of tinkering represent the theoretical framework of the activity, where, manually exploring a problem, various kinds of objects are being made using recycled materials [6], also according to the principles of the Russian psychologist Lev Vygotsky [27] who considered such types of activities useful for expanding children's minds. Just like him, we, too, have found inspiration by the perspective in the 19th century pedagogue Freire's work [13] who used children's intelligence and inventiveness as potential drives for transformation. After completing the activity, we analyzed it in order to understand how children have progressively addressed environmental concerns, as a reflection in terms of social capital [1, 18], starting from the manual dialogue with the materials and culminating with building useful artefacts [20].

2   Collapse Informatics

Over the past years, the concept of collapse has started to become more and more familiar to people as they often hear it in the media (e.g. [9]). A society collapses when it loses economic, environmental, and social resources, thus leading to the excessive poverty of its people [9]. Many important past cultures are described by historians during their greatness, during their road towards collapse, and often all the way to their complete disappearance. The interest to understand why so many social systems have collapsed in the past also helps us to understand the current behaviour of industrialized civilizations, especially those that recklessly exploit our natural resources, pollute, or are overpopulated. As a result of those historical analyses, we can direct our current stance towards sustainable choices that would hopefully prevent us, the humanity, from becoming extinct. The concept of collapse has been adapted to the HCI discipline thus coining the term of collapse informatics (e.g. [25, 26]), which encloses reflective practices that overall challenge societal trends such as mass production, disposable culture, planned obsolescence, and consumerism. This is where the tinkering practices come in handy given that they promote the reuse of waste and its re-semantization into novel contexts and for different uses. Customization, creativity, reuse, and design-in-use are some processes involved in constructivism and DIY practices. Configurability, visibility, subversion, openness, interpretation and intentionality are a few features of those newly built objects [7, 23]. Those new objects tell the story of their past life and engage with the user in a journey in which function, material qualities, aesthetic pleasure, and interpretation are all embodied in new artefacts [16]. This is called the concept of domestication [8] that speaks of the ability of the new objects to modify the environments they are located in and to inspire a sense of ownership and affection in their owner.

3   The Work of Vladimir Archipov

The Russian photographer, Archipov, travelled across post-soviet Russia for 11 years while documenting homemade artefacts [2]. His artistic and anthropological considerations and his views on recycle and reuse are extremely relevant for this paper.

The starting point of his research is the shortage of goods in the post-soviet Russia. We started this project driven by the shortage of resources due to extensive use and mirrored his findings. He shot marvellous homemade objects and gathered information about their building process, thereby representing the private daily life in a country where the lack of goods was a day-to-day problem. DIY, in turn, provided feelings of pride, satisfaction and ownership for the home made artefacts effectiveness and unicity. In fact, even if those objects are far from being perfectly executed like those done by professionals, they represent the transformation of an object into another, transformation which, in itself, is an artistic process. In his photographs, we can find tools for processing food, for taking care of bee hives, for carpentering, for gardening, for fishing, for skiing, for making music, or toys for children to play with. Those objects are often meant to increase the quality of life of their owners, like an antenna made up of forks that helps its owner and creator to catch TV programs. Due to the militarization of the soviet regime, many object were made of materials from military equipment. The DIY culture in his book often comes is rooted in his ancestor's skills to build useful objects for sport, leisure or hobbies that they would not have been able to own otherwise. This usually made people revalue leftover materials, such as plastic, wood, metal and appreciate them for their intrinsic properties, e.g. resistance, malleability, isolating capacity, lightness, transparency, etc. Those objects hold their intelligence and their unicity out from marketing. At the same time, we believe that those objects belong to the field of research through design in that they are diegetic artefacts, objects that tell a story and concretize the imaginary of the person that built them from waste. Following that, there is a brief review of some of the critical stances in HCI that we took inspiration from for our workshop with the children.

4   The Diegetic Artefacts

Collapse informatics, as part of the HCI theory, is a reflective practice aimed at articulating compelling sustainability issues. In this context, reflectivity materializes the design concern unveiling sustainability issues and bringing them to the public attention. Critical reflection takes, indeed, a political stance when designers are asked to focus on everyday practices and deal with prejudiced mindsets that view certain things as garbage and [20] identify alternatives to those practices. Those reflections can be included in the broad category of research through design, too [28] since they uses design methods in order to explore, code, understand, and present problem spaces, facilitating their perception from different perspectives. This is achieved by manipulating the elements involved, creating novel combinations, and providing unusual views on a topic. For example, design fictions [24] have been proposed as unconventional prototypes describing imaginary tomorrows and creating bewilderment toward otherwise familiar topics. This process of defamiliarization is not new to the HCI's theory [3, 5]. Estrangement is a creative method of opening up design spaces by disconnecting from familiar experiences and looking at the usual context with a form of 'disorientation'. In this framework, diegetic artefacts provide the tangible materialization of these feelings. On the one hand, diegetic artefacts are objects on the borderline between literary practice and design that help us to visualize alternative futures. On the other hand, this activity, should encourage people to reflectively and critically view the present days. Design prototypes incorporate meanings, values, narratives, feelings, threats and it has even poetic aspects, thus, enabling a creative manipulation of the assumptions hidden in the status quo. This way, they physically bring utopias or dystopias to reality while ideologically questioning the present through design practice [11]. In the context of our case studies, we have made particular use of diegetic prototypes, in which fiction is incorporated into physical artefacts, thus assuming a diegetic feature. These prototypes imply the imagined world in which they function, a world that is explained and concretized thanks to the narrative qualities of the designed objects. These artefacts establish the contexts and conditions in which they take place and they create the scenario for moving back and forth between the present and the future, thus, anticipating a playful discussion on ethics, values, and implications. All these paradigms are an important source of inspiration for our work. Another important part of the theory concerns the creative approach towards children and the use of imagination to transmit them values, thoughts and reflections on sustainable design.

5   The Work of Paulo Freire and the Constructivism

The exploration of materials and the free manual dialogue with them [14, 20] have important roots in the past of educational theory. The pedagogical work of Freire, for example, is aimed at presenting an educational framework in which the child actively creates his own existential and cultural growth [13]. In Freire's opinion, knowledge exists only in invention and re-invention, in the restless and permanent questioning of the world and of other people, where the teacher does not fill his pupils with notions but is a facilitator of research processes that lead to discovering those notions themselves. This way, learning takes place during activities of joint re-creation and transformation of the existing realities, in order to make sense of them. This method emphasizes the uniqueness of children through creativity, valuing their humanity and their conscience through an intentional relationship with the world. This problem-based learning becomes a joint activity involving both the pupils and the teacher, in which challenges become a vehicle for critical knowledge and, in turn, an expansion of the mental frameworks. This develops a set of strategies to know the unknown in children that is Freire's main message. The pedagogue believes that education must be more like learning to discover rather than having the contents delivered by the teacher. Thus, pupils are actively involved in their learning processes which is also the main tenet of constructivism and is explained as follows.

5.1   The Constructivism

The term constructivism has its has been built upon Papert's experience of using ICT with children [17, 19] and focuses on the active exploration of a topic, while linking what is being discovered with existing knowledge and experience. Constructivism refers to the constructivist theory of Piaget who considers learning as a reconstruction of knowledge and not just as a simple transmission of that knowledge. Accordingly, the construction and therefore the learning is more effective and mastered when it is not only mental, but it is supported by a real construction, by an activity such as the building of a meaningful project. Thus, constructivism introduces the construct of cognitive artefacts: objects or devices that support learning as an external framework that allows the internal and correspondent creation of knowledge. These concrete products must be shown, discussed, examined, probed, and shared. Therefore, children develop their own understanding of the world as an active process of building. This way, they autonomously acquire knowledge by expanding their own frameworks. The child becomes the protagonist of learning, while the teacher assumes the role of a facilitator, who should refrain from providing pre-build solutions; he, instead, must try to help the pupils to follow their own paths toward personal, meaningful goals. Another important point is the peers collaboration as a relevant method to interactively achieving shared goals. This particular emphasis on external activities and collective goals is linked to the vygotskian construct of knowledge that stipulates that one should first develop using elements of the outside world and then through inner cognition [27]. An important method for putting these ideas into practice is tinkering, the child's manual, creative exploration of a topic with the final aim of expanding his personal, mental frameworks.

5.2 Tinkering

Children's making of objects is receiving substantial attention in the educational field and gaining more and more weight on its agenda (e.g. [4, 19]). In particular, tinkering is highly valued for its capacity to trigger imagination, exploration tendencies, and critical thinking, whilst allowing children to make mistakes and learn from them. The activity of tinkering implies the free experimentation with raw materials without always having a precise aim in mind and it is directed toward developing a detachment from a consumerist attitude [6]. By manually exploring materials, children take control of their own creative processes, learn to take risks, to come up with rules and, at times, even break them, in order to expand their individuality and their sense of self [6]. Through tinkering, children gradually develop autonomy, freedom and responsibility, which, in turn, allow them to develop feelings of ownership and affection toward the built objects. Therefore, making becomes a method for the children to have a primary role in their own education and to empower themselves in order to look at the world with novel perspectives and, why not, eventually change it. Tinkering fosters artistic expression, subversion, as well as producing, contributing enhancing, extending, changing, and re-creating reality [6]. In this context, we made use of tinkering with recycled materials in order to develop environmental consciousness and an ecological concern.

6 The Activity

We carried out the activity with twenty primary school children aged 9–11. In order to include the topic of smart city and in particularly that of environmental sustainability, we encouraged the pupils to use recycled materials and computational components. The activity was funded by the Department for Equal Opportunities of the Italian

Government, was designed to increase children's skills in STEM (Science, Technology, Engineering and Mathematics) and took place during a summer school (40 h). The activity is a part of a two-year project whose ultimate goal is to imagine the elements of the neighbourhood of the future using a "smart" perspective, through the design of "intelligent objects" that can respond to specific energy and environmental needs (pollution, waste collection, etc.). In the first year, in which the activities described were carried out, the theme of environmental sustainability, typical for smart cities, and the importance of garbage separate collection were conducted with the help of workshops based on Tinkering and Making. The children watched videos about recycling and the re-use of objects, about how materials can be reused, and the new object we create with it take on a new function in order to avoid waste, thus, optimizing the resources - that are not infinite (e.g. new bicycles made of recycled aluminium cans). Can waste be reused to create new objects? Can we design new objects, machines that can help us with waste and resource management? These we two of the questions to which the pupils answered affirmatively when they came up with pupil new robots that respond to specific needs in terms of environmental sustainability: for example robots that drive independently and clean the streets of waste; a drone that waters only when it recognizes a dry flowerbed, a robot that collects waste and empties bins; an intelligent box with sensors to facilitate opening it by people with disabilities. Each child has, therefore, drew/designed his own robot in their notebook, has individuated the constituent parts, the materials to be used, the functions that the robot can perform, and has created a model. Then the children were explained the notions of "smart" object, computational power, algorithms and following instructions and then each child reflected on that. In order to test how much the pupils have understood, technological kits (Lego WeDo 2.0) have been used, Lego bricks with which to build machines or robots that can move and perform actions thanks to sensors and components programmable with Lego or Scratch APP software. These software packages are based on block programming languages and allow the pupils to approach typical coding concepts, creating algorithms, using instruction sequences, conditional cycles (If.. then.. else), iterative (Do... while) to make their object move. The overall activity followed the basic steps of design and implementation, but the focus of the activity was the tinkering process.

6.1 Analyzing the Activity

Four week after the completion of the activity, we administered the 20 children a questionnaire. Its purpose was to evaluate it and find out the opinion of children about recycling after what we consider to be a significant amount of time for the information to settle in the mind of a child. Overall, the quantitative analysis of the multiple choice questions reveals appreciation of the activity. The children did not find the activity neither difficult nor out of the ordinary and this was interesting to us. The qualitative analysis of the questionnaire shows some other aspects. For example, when we asked the children to describe their robot and to write a little reflection on recycling in order for us to understand if this practice had influenced the children's environmental awareness, their thoughts were sometimes vague, but overall, they showed some understanding of the usefulness of recycling.

"I think I will recycle every time." [N19]

"If we learn how to properly recycle we will maintain the world clean." [N20]

Other times, the awareness of material savings is more defined and developed, revealing a growing awareness for the ecological goal of the activity.

"To me, recycling is very important and objects should not be misused." [N09]

"Recycling materials is useful for the cities of the future, but also to spare trees, oil, gasoline, etc." [N12]

"If we recycle, we will maintain the world clean and we will save money." [N16]

They felt the activity as playful and they loved to learn new things and be with their peers; they perceived the environmental awareness as an important thing to posses.

"I like to recycle because waste can become much more than just waste" [N05]

"I've learned how important it is to recycle and how many good things you can create with waste." [N13]

During the activity, children learned to look at waste from a different perspective and were able to choose the suitable materials for the robot's anatomical parts they had to build. This new meaning attribution to waste materials was the central core of our activity, because during this interaction with materials children were able to achieve an abstract perception of environmental consciousness. Moreover, the robot functions are closer to the children's daily life, as we can see in the following excerpts from the transcripts of the discussions with our young participants.

"[my robot] has the body made from a plastic bottle, the eyes made with two corks, it has a light over the head, its purpose is to illuminate a room during the night." [N14]

"My robot has to collect metal from the ground. It has two magnets as hand. I have made it using a milk box, two paper rolls, a box, and two magnets." [N15]

When we asked them for suggestions on how to improve the activity, they understood that the question referred to recycling and they wrote sort of slogans like:

"Before throwing away an object think what you could make from that broken object. In two words: recycle it!" [N04].

Overall, the children's answers reveal that they had a positive experience, they enjoyed taking part in a creative activity based on making, and they showed greater sensitivity to the environment.

7 Discussion

The children participating in this activity were encouraged with this activity, we allowed the children to use their knowledge and skills to build something creative that came from their ingenious minds. Designing a robot was perceived as a game, but in fact it was an acquisition experience in a learning context where children not only used the skills they already possessed but acquired new ones on the topic of environmental sustainability, the value of recycling, and correct waste management, on the one hand and project work and relating hypotheses and solutions, on the other. When reconstructing the activity, we realized that we let them reflect, in a playful context, on the future consequences of current waste management actions. Moreover, the children's diegetic prototypes [24] told stories of sustainability through reuse, so they used the design activity as a tool to support imagination, knowledge, reasoning and interpretation. In this in a general sense, their visual and tactile dialogue with the recycled materials represented a *reflection-in-action* activity [20] that captured the physicality, fascination and specific features of the objects, which in turn made them realize the value of waste and the importance of its good use. With this activity, children were introduced to the DIY philosophy which is the base principle of collapse informatics; they were involved in the reconfiguration of discarded objects that acquired novel meanings by being assembled and repurposed. This can be considered not only a creative activity, but also has specific aspects of intentionality and subversion. Furthermore, the adaptation of waste materials to new contexts also allowed their creators to establish an affective relationship with them, through feelings of ownership and aesthetic pleasure. The main idea was that the material dialogue [14, 20] with the objects discarded by the parents and reused by the children was a playful way to develop the internalization of recycling value in a social context. This idea, in turn, is consistent with Vygotsky's interplay between inter-psychic (socialized psychological structures in a collective environment) and the intra-psychic categories (when children develop those structures starting from their own) [27]. Reflection in action [20], in this case, represents a conversation with the materials [14]. Their manipulation, the movement back and forth from the particular to the general, i.e. from the physicality to the intrinsic features of the waste materials, leads to a deeper appreciation of their existing qualities that can expend in order to re-contextualize household waste in novel contexts and with new functions. Therefore, making, in this case, stimulates a reflection about the renewable objects, representing in turn an expansion of existing mental frameworks toward overcoming the throwaway culture and the assumption of new positions of sustainable design. Recycling activity can be referred to the theory of Social Capital [1, 18]. The core structure of Social Capital consists in an individual's sense of belonging to a community in which there is a mutual benefit coming from all those who have certain behaviours. In this case study, children were asked to develop Social Capital by recycling waste materials in order to save them and prevent their scarcity in the future.

8 Conclusion

The described activity was aimed at activating and strengthening children's feeling of belonging to the community and life skills, while addressing the issue of environmental sustainability with ICT. The main goal of this summer school project was to design a sustainable "smart" city by addressing the environmental and energy issues of the present with the help of technologies of a near future. We approached our goals from a constructivist view point, asking the children to tackle problems in a playful and creative manner through tinkering. Firstly, every child imagined a computational object, and then made a prototype of that object with household waste; each of them decided autonomously the robot's shape and behaviour. This allowed us to introduce the issues of environmental sustainability, the importance of waste separation and the possibility to transform an object into another one with a different function. As a second step, the children shared their results with their peers in a group activity and received suggestions. The teamwork activities was also increased their social and communicative skills and their confidence in collective, creative processes. The final goal of the activity was to stimulate creativity, reflection, and a positive attitude towards sustainability. The results we gathered can give us some valuable insights for tackling environmental issues, which could be valuable for the whole HCI community as well as. DIY activities with the goal of reflecting on sustainability are critical-thinking activities in which children have reasoned about their own future and about the world that adults are leaving them. The described activity belongs to the area of HCI called research through design [28] through which we provided children with tools and procedures for critically analyzing the present and the future in relation to the current activity of waste management. We chose a tinkering activity because it is a hands-on, trial, and error-based learning process that encourages experimentation, team work, and cooperative learning in an informal environment. By exploiting creativity, manual skills and curiosity, pupils were able to develop skills that are fundamental in the contemporary world, such as critical thinking and the ability to innovate, they also learn to learn and increase their desire for lifelong learning. DIY activities enrich training programs with soft skills (communication and team working skills, problem solving and design thinking) and help to acquire life skills, for example citizen identity, as in the case study we presented above. The activity was not only aimed at allowing children to invent, but also at giving them the opportunity to reflect on the environment. This was possible by challenging the current situation (the abundance of waste) and finding alternatives (doing something useful with it). At the same time, we have stimulated skills like design thinking, reflecting on the future consequences of current/present behaviour, thinking about technologies (and their possible applications in daily life), civic engagement, and the development of ethical reasoning about the current situation. Children learned life skills related to the environmental sustainability, the importance of recycling, and the proper waste management all done in a playful way. Moreover, they acquired problem solving skills, they learnt how to carry on a project step by step, and how to test their own hypotheses and find possible solutions. To sum up, they strengthen their civic engagement, ethical reasoning, innovation skills, critical attitude, and team work.

References

1. Adler, P.S., Know, S.-W.: Social capital: prospects for a new concept. Acad. Manage. Rev. **27**(1), 17–40 (2002)
2. Arkhipov, V.: Home-Made: Contemporary Russian Folk Artifacts. FUEL Publishing, London (2006)
3. Bell, G., Blythe, M., Sengers, P.: Making by making strange: defamiliarization and the design of domestic technologies. ACM TOCHI12 **2**, 149–173 (2005)
4. Blikstein, P.: Maker movement in education: history and prospects. In: de Vries, M.J. (ed.) Handbook of Technology Education. Springer, New York. (2018)
5. Carlson, K., Schiphorst, T.: Designing interaction for designers: defamiliarization in user's creative decision-making. In: C&C 2013. ACM (2013)
6. Cermak-Sassenrath, D., Møllenbach, E.: Teaching to tinker: making as an educational strategy. In: NordiCHI 2014, pp. 789–792. ACM, New York (2014)
7. Desjardins, A., Wakkary, R.: Manifestations of everyday design: guiding goals and motivations. In: C&C 2013, Sydney, Australia, 17–20 June 2013 (2013)
8. Dix, A.: Designing for appropriation. In: British HCI Group Annual Conference on People and Computers, Swindon, UK, 03–07 September 2007 (2007)
9. Diamond, J.: Collapse: How Societies Choose to Fail or Succeed. Pinguin (2001)
10. Dunne, A., Raby, F.: Design Noir: The Secret Life of Electronic Objects. Birkhäuser, Basel (2001)
11. Dunne, A.: Hertzian Tales: Electronic Products, Aesthetic Experience, and Critical Design. The MIT Press, Cambridge (2005)
12. Dunne, A., Raby, F.: Speculative Everything: Design, Fiction, and Social Dreaming. The MIT Press, Boston (2013)
13. Freire, P.: Pedagogy of the Oppressed. Revised edition. Penguin Books, London (1993)
14. Ingold, T.: On weaving a basket. The Perception of the Environment: Essays on Livelihood Dwelling and Skill, pp. 339–348. Routledge, London (2000)
15. Nardi, B.: Designing for the future: but which one? Interactions **23**(1), 26–33 (2015)
16. Odom, W., Pierce, J., Stolterman, E., Blevis, E.: Understanding why we preserve some things and discard others in the context of interaction design. In: CHI 2009, Boston, MA, 04–09 April 2009 (2009)
17. Papert, S., Harel, I. (Eds.) Constructionism. The MIT Press (1991)
18. Putnam, R.D.: Democracies in Flux: The Evolution of Social Capital in Contemporary Society. Oxford University Press, New York (2002)
19. Resnick, M.: Lifelong Kindergarten: Cultivating Creativity Through Projects, Passion, Peers, and Play. The MIT Press, Cambridge (2017)
20. Schön, D.A.: The Reflective Practitioner: How Professionals Think in Action. Temple Smith, London (1983)
21. Sengers, P., Boehner, K., David, S., Kaye, J.: Reflective design. In: AARHUS 2005, pp. 49–58, Århus, Denmark, 21–25 August 2005 (2005)
22. Tanenbaum, J., Tanenbaum, K., Wakkary, R.: Design fictions. In: TEI 2012, Kingston, Ontario, Canada, 19–22 February 2012 (2012)
23. Tanenbaum, J.G., Williams, A.M., Desjardins, A., Tanenbaum, K.: Democratizing technology: pleasure, utility and expressiveness in DIY and maker practice. In: CHI 2013, Paris, France, 27 April–02 May 2013 (2013)
24. Tanenbaum, J.: Design fictional interactions: why HCI should care about stories. Interactions **21**(5), 22–23 (2014)

25. Tomlinson, B., Silberman, M.S., Patterson, D., Pan, Y., Blevis, E.: Collapse informatics: augmenting the sustainability & ICT4D discourse in HCI. In: CHI 2012, Austin, Texas, 05–10 May, 2012 (2012)
26. Tomlinson, B., Blevis, E., Nardi, B., Patterson, D.J., Silberman, M.S., Pan, Y.: Collapse informatics and practice: theory, method, and design. ACM TOCHI **20**(4), 1–26 (2013)
27. Wertsch, J.V.: Vygotsky and the Social Formation of Mind. Harvard University Press, Cambridge (1988)
28. Zimmerman, J., Forlizzi, J., Evenson, S.: Research through design as a method for interaction design research in HCI. In: Proceedings of the SIGCHI Conference on Human Factors in Computing Systems (CHI 2007). ACM, New York (2007)

"Play and Learn": Exploring CodeCubes

Bárbara Cleto[1]([⊠]) [iD], Cristina Sylla[2] [iD], Luís Ferreira[1] [iD],
and João Martinho Moura[1] [iD]

[1] Escola Superior de Tecnologia, Instituto Politécnico do Cávado e do Ave,
Barcelos, Portugal
al3993@alunos.ipca.pt, {lufer, jmoura}@ipca.pt
[2] Research Centre on Child Studies, Universidade do Minho, Braga, Portugal
cristina.sylla@ie.uminho.pt

Abstract. This paper presents a study carried out with a group of students from a robotic club, where they have used CodeCubes, a hybrid interface that combines physical paper cubes with Augmented Reality (AR). CodeCubes, intends to promote computational thinking through exploration and experimentation. The intervention, which we report here aimed at assessing children's interest and motivation for these types of interfaces, as well as identifying possible interaction difficulties with CodeCubes. The results indicate that the children were motivated to work with CodeCubes, and that the physicality of the interface combined with AR can potentially promote hands-on learning.

Keywords: Interaction · Augmented reality · Computational thinking · Tangible interfaces

1 Introduction

The Hour of Code is a global movement that attracts millions of students in over 180 countries [1], taking place once a year all over the world. The event has the duration of one hour and consists of programming activities that aim at demystifying programming and showing that everyone can learn the basics of programming. Further, the Hour of Code aims at attracting students to the field. A similar event, the Code Week, which is sponsored by the European Commission, takes place once a year all over Europe. It is conceived as "a grass-roots movement that celebrates creativity, problem solving and collaboration through programming and other tech activities" [2]. Such initiatives demonstrate well the importance of creating environments and materials targeting a wide audience, independently of age and previous programming knowledge, to promote the learning of the basic principles of computational thinking in an intuitive and compelling way. Outgoing from this context, we developed CodeCubes, a hybrid interface that combines physical paper cubes with AR technology.

The CodeCubes' game mechanic was inspired by a game from the Code.org platform [3], namely, Angry Birds - Classic Maze [4]. These types of games are often used to introduce programming to novice students. In the Code.org platform the players use visual programming through drag and drop to program and overcome challenges. In CodeCubes the visual programming blocks are replaced by physical paper blocks.

C. Sylla and I. Iurgel (Eds.): TIE 2019, LNICST 307, pp. 34–42, 2020.
https://doi.org/10.1007/978-3-030-40180-1_4

Each face of each block has an augmented reality (AR) marker that triggers the basic programming instructions: right, left, up and down. The player must program a car to follow a defined path using these four instructions. This study aimed at investigating if and to which extent AR and tangible technology can be an effective complement in educational settings, as well to identify possible interaction difficulties with Code-Cubes. The study was carried out with a group of children aged between nine and thirteen years of age that have experience with programming with blocks, i.e. Scratch [5] and robotics. None of the participants was familiar with AR.

2 Background

Augmented reality refers to the integration of virtual and real information, processed in real time. AR interfaces allow controlling and visualizing the information according to the users' needs [6]. Instead of replacing the reality [7], AR interfaces complement it, augmenting and superimposing the virtual information on the real world, without providing a complete immersion. This way, creating an interactive environment where the real is strengthened with virtual information in real time [8]. The use of AR in educational settings allows interacting with information, objects or 3D events in a more natural way [8, 9]. This enables the users - often with a high level of realism [11, 13] – to interact with the real world in a novel way. E.g., manipulating virtual objects and/or observing phenomena that are difficult to observe or manipulate in the real world, for instance, visualization, exploration and manipulation of the human body [20]. This technology also allows creating learning environments that combine virtual and real objects [11], e.g., using tangible interfaces for the manipulation of virtual objects, [8, 9]. Tangible user interfaces (TUIs) are physical objects embedded with computational properties that allow manipulating digital content [20, 21]. These interfaces create a seamless interaction between the virtual and the real and make it possible to change between both worlds. AR environments have three components: (i) combination of the real and the virtual world, (ii) real time interaction (iii) being inserted in a 3D environment [7].

The interaction and immersion made possible by AR has the potential to motivate the students and increase their willingness to learn [11, 13–15]. Studies have shown that the integration of AR in educational settings has a positive effect, increasing motivation, students' interaction and collaboration [10]. Relatively to the challenges of using AR in such settings these are mainly associated with usability issues and technical problems [11]. Same students may also find the technology difficult to use [11, 16] and the combination of real and virtual objects may create confusion [11, 12]. Some of these difficulties may as well be a result from poor interface design [11, 16]. However, overall the easiness of use of AR is considered an advantage [11, 16]. The involvement of educators in the design of such interfaces may help overcome difficulties of use and facilitate the integration of AR in educational settings [11, 13], although it may take some time to overcome these difficulties [11, 15].

3   CodeCubes

CodeCubes allows physical programming and virtual representation of the generated program. The users manipulate physical paper cubes that have an AR marker on each face, which is associated with a programming instruction and can be used to overcome a set of challenges. The programming, which is carried out through the physical manipulation of the cubes, allows its simultaneous visualization. This allows changing the program while it is running and visualizing the changes while the program is running. This approach to programming potentially promotes an interactive and engaging experience [19]. The game has three levels and consists of controlling a car to travel a pre-determined trajectory and reach the goal (see Fig. 1). The trajectory and the car are displayed on the computer screen.

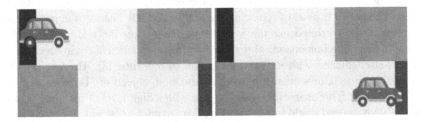

Fig. 1. Game elements (trajectory and the car) – level 1.

In order to reach the goal, the user has to program a sequence of actions that brings the car from the start to the end of the trajectory. In order to trigger these movements and make the car move forward in the right direction, the player needs to place the AR marker representing the required instruction (right, left, up, down) in front of the camera (See Fig. 2). The movements of the car are visualized on the computer screen.

Fig. 2. A participant using CodeCubes.

The car moves forward, according to the programming instructions, until reaching the end line. The player can progress by running the code step by step or programming the whole sequence (see Figs. 3 and 4).

In case the player is unable to program the instructions correctly but manages to bring the car to the end line s/he can move to the next level. The game is over when the three levels are completed. However, the users can always return to a previous level. The performance is measured by the time that the users need to reach the goal. This approach intends to motivate the students to learn how to program and to explore different possibilities.

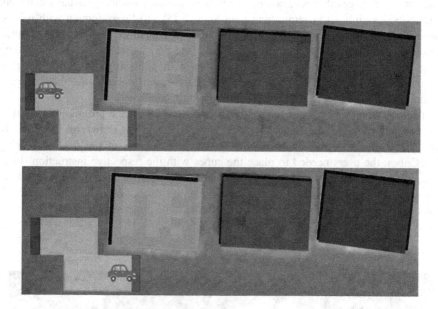

Fig. 3. The car trajectory

4 Exploratory Study

We carried out an exploratory study to (i) understand if the use of a tangible pedagogical resource combined with AR motivates and engages the students to carry out programming activities, (ii) to identify possible difficulties of use of CodeCubes, (iii) to gather ideas for future developments of CodeCubes.

4.1 Study Context

The intervention was carried out in a robotic club. The sessions took place during the opening times of the club, which is open daily from 6.30 PM till 7.30 PM. The students usually create projects using Scratch [5], as well as robotics' projects that are related to the school curriculum. We received written informed consent from the participants' parents.

4.2   Participants and Procedure

Nine students aged between nine and thirteen years of age, with an average of ten years, participated in the intervention. Four were male and five female. None of the participants was familiar with AR. The study lasted six weeks and comprised one hourly session per week, six sessions in total.

In order to find out if the students were motivated to use CodeCubes, it was compared with three other programming activities that the participants usually carry out in the robotics club, (i) Programming with Scratch [5], (ii) Programming with robots, and (iii) Programming with the Code.org platform [3, 4]. All the students programmed the same task using each of the three platforms (see Fig. 1), namely, (i) programming using visual programming blocks (programing with software) (Scratch); (ii), programming a Lego WeDo® robot to carry out the same trajectory as the car (programming with hardware); (iii) programming with CodeCubes.

The trajectory was pre-defined, and was the same for all the programming activities. For programming the Lego WeDo® robot the track was drawn on the floor. In order to program the car to move from the start to the end of the trajectory using CodeCubes, the users needed to place the cubes with the respective instruction (face) facing the devices' camera. However, the camera sometimes captured two faces of the cubes, which generated some confusion among the users. To avoid this, we have replaced the paper cubes by paper squares with the same dimensions as each face of the physical paper cubes (Fig. 4).

Fig. 4. A participant testing and running the program (top).

Similarly, to program with Scratch the participants had to use the visual blocks (using drag and drop) to program the car to move from start to the end of the trajectory.

The first session was dedicated to the presentation of the activities and the collection of demographic data. In session two and three the participants freely explored CodeCubes and carried out the tasks for each of the three levels. In session four and five each participant carried out following tasks individually (i) programming with CodeCubes; (ii) programming the car to follow the track using Scratch; (iii) programming the Lego WeDo® robot to walk the same track as the car. In session six each participant was interviewed individually.

In summary, in order to compare and evaluate children's preferences towards each of the programming methods the participants carried out the same task using three different approaches. The final task was carried out in the Code.Org [3] platform for playing Angry Birds - Classic Maze [4].

4.3   Data Collection

In order to understand children's engagement and interest, the data collection was carried out through direct observation, field notes, photographs and video recordings. The demographic data was collected through questionnaires. In order to assess children's preferences and experience with the different programming modalities, a questionnaire was applied before the intervention, after using CodeCubes and at the end of the intervention.

The questionnaire was composed of four sections. Section one collected demographic data, section two collected children's opinion about CodeCubes, section three concerned children's opinion about using AR in class, and section four asked the children to evaluate the activities carried out during the intervention using a five-pointsLikert scale. In the last session each participant was interviewed individually. This interview aimed to clarify and confirm some of the information collected through direct observation.

4.4   Observations and Discussion

We observed that the participants did not show difficulties using the physical AR markers to program the proposed tasks. They followed an exploratory approach, by trial and error being able to carry out the proposed tasks. To accomplish the first level most participants executed the code instruction by instruction instead of using the ordered sequence of instructions. However, in the following levels they programmed the whole sequence.

We observed that the participants were engaged and motivated to carry out the proposed tasks, actively solving them. This was confirmed by their answers to the questionnaire and the interviews. Table 1 displays section two of the questionnaire (ease of use).

Table 1. Section two of the questionnaire - CodeCubes, ease of use.

Question	Yes	No	Some
Did you need help to use CodeCubes?		8	1
Does CodeCubes require long to learn how to use it?		9	
Did you enjoy using CodeCubes?	9		

Concerning the level of difficulty, eight participants considered CodeCubes easy to use and did not need help to use it. All referred that it did not take long to learn it. All the participants enjoyed using CodeCubes.

After accomplishing the four tasks, the participants evaluated the activities developed using a five-points Likert scale with following classification 1-not like; 2-like a little; 3- no opinion; 4-like; 5-like very much). The results are presented on Table 2.

Table 2. Section 4 of the questionnaire displaying the rating of the activities

Activity	Ratings (five- points Likert Scale)				
	1	2	3	4	5
Programming the robot		1	1	2	5
Programming with scratch	1	1		2	5
Programming with AR (CodeCubes)				2	7
Programming with Code.org	1		2	1	5

Seven participants rated CodeCubes with 5 (like very much), and two rated it with 4 (like). Most of the participants, also liked to program the robot, scratch and code.org, rating these activities with a five, (like very much). Since the results for all the activities were very similar, we applied another questionnaire to the participants asking them which activities they preferred most. We used a 4 points scale with following classification: 1-not like; 2-like a little; 3-like; 4-like very much). The results showed that eight out of nine participants preferred the programming with AR (CodeCubes) activity, see Table 3.

Table 3. Section 4 of the questionnaire representing the preferred activities.

Activity	Ratings			
	1	2	3	4
Programming the robot		2	4	3
Programming with scratch	1	1	5	2
Programming with AR (CodeCubes)		1		8
Programming with Code.org	1	2	4	2

In the interview the students referred that they like to assemble the robot and to program it, as well as to see if it carries out the programmed instructions. Most of them said that they gave the robot a nickname and that they gave it orders while programming it (as if they were communicating with the robots). This "communication" did not happen when they were programming with Scratch or using the Code.org platform. Regarding the CodeCubes, the students referred that it was new for them and that they enjoyed manipulating the paper markers and simultaneously see their hands while programming. They especially liked to see the virtual elements overlay the real and to be able to control the visual elements through the physical manipulation of objects.

In the interviews we also asked the participants to tell us which changes they would apply to CodeCubes. They referred that they would like to have more characters and audio. A girl suggested that the challenge could be to have a character that would collect trash, which would increase in higher levels. The aim of the game would be to collect as much trash as possible to fill a trash bin. A boy mentioned that he would like to have scores. All the participants expressed their wish to use CodeCubes in class, and that it could also be integrated in schoolbooks.

5 Conclusions

We have described an intervention carried out with nine students in a robotics club. The intervention aimed at assessing the potential of CodeCubes for motivating the students, as well as possible interaction difficulties. CodeCubes was easy to start with for all the participants, they have enjoyed all the activities and CodeCubes above all.

The participants were very engaged and carried out the proposed tasks enthusiastically. The results confirmed previous research about the potential of tangibles and AR as a pedagogical tool that potentially promotes the student's motivation and engagement, which may lead to increased learning [13, 17, 18].

6 Limitations and Future Work

The results presented in this study are confined to a very restricted universe, therefore they are merely indicative. The participation of a larger number of students, in a long-term study, would be needed to further confirm the results presented here.

Due to usability issues, instead of using the physical paper cubes the students preferred to use paper pieces. In future work we will explore different possibilities in order to find a better solution for the detection of the cubes' faces by the camera. The suggestions provided by the participants, e.g., to add audio, a range of different characters as well as a punctuation system will help to improve the system. We will also create more levels and a new set of instructions using structures, loops and selection.

Another interesting possibility that we are considering is to implement a multi-player version to extend the group interaction. This would potentially allow investigating to which extent the AR technology may contribute to develop prosocial behavior.

Acknowledgments. We thank the participants and their parents from the Robotics programming club for their participation in the study and for their valuable suggestions.

References

1. Hour of code. https://hourofcode.com. Accessed 10 June 2019
2. Code Week. https://codeweek.eu/. Accessed 10 June 2019
3. Code.org: What will you create?. https://code.org/learn. Accessed 10 June 2019
4. Angry Birds - Code.org - Classic Maze. https://studio.code.org/hoc/1. Accessed 10 June 2019
5. Scratch Online. https://scratch.mit.edu/. Accessed 10 June 2019

6. Liarokapis, F., Macan, L., Malone, G., Rebolledo-Mendez, G., De Freitas, S.: A pervasive augmented reality serious game. In: 2009 Conference in Games and Virtual Worlds for Serious Applications, pp. 148–155. IEEE, March 2009
7. Azuma, R.T.: A survey of augmented reality. Teleoperators Virtual Environ. **6**(4), 355–385 (1997)
8. Kesim, M., Ozarslan, Y.: Augmented reality in education: current technologies and the potential for education. Procedia-Soc. Behav. Sci. **47**, 297–302 (2012)
9. Billinghurst, M.: Augmented Reality in Education. New Horizons for Learning – Technology in Education, Seattle (2002)
10. Bacca, J., Baldiris, S., Fabregat, R., Graf, S.: Augmented reality trends in education: a systematic review of research and applications. Educ. Technol. Soc. **17**, 133–149 (2014)
11. Khan, T., Johnston, K., Ophoff, J.: The impact of an augmented reality application on learning motivation of students. Adv. Hum. Comput. Interact. **2019**, 14 (2019)
12. Wu, H.K., Lee, S.W.Y., Chang, H.Y., Liang, J.C.: Current status, opportunities and challenges of augmented reality in education. Comput. Educ. **62**, 41–49 (2013)
13. Wei, X., Weng, D., Liu, Y., Wang, Y.: Teaching based on augmented reality for a technical creative design course. Comput. Educ. **81**, 221–234 (2015)
14. Di Serio, Á., Ibáñez, M.B., Kloos, C.D.: Impact of an augmented reality system on students' motivation for a visual art course. Comput. Educ. **68**, 586–596 (2013)
15. Gopalan, V., Zulkifli, A.N., Bakar, J.A.A.: A study of students' motivation using the augmented reality science textbook. In: AIP Conference Proceedings, vol. 1761, no. 1, p. 020040. AIP Publishing, August 2016
16. Akçayır, M., Akçayır, G.: Advantages and challenges associated with augmented reality for education: a systematic review of the literature. Educ. Res. Rev. **20**, 1–11 (2017)
17. Lu, S.J., Liu, Y.C.: Integrating augmented reality technology to enhance children's learning in marine education. Environ. Educ. Res. **21**(4), 525–541 (2015)
18. Cheng, K.H., Tsai, C.C.: Children and parents' reading of an augmented reality picture book: analyses of behavioral patterns and cognitive attainment. Comput. Educ. **72**, 302–312 (2014)
19. Cabrera, L., Maloney, J.H., Weintrop, D.: Programs in the palm of your hand: how live programming shapes children's interactions with physical computing devices. In: Proceedings of the 18th ACM International Conference on Interaction Design and Children, pp. 227–236. ACM, June 2019
20. Hornecker, E., Buur, J.: Getting a grip on tangible interaction: a framework on physical space and social interaction. In: Proceedings of the SIGCHI Conference on Human Factors in Computing Systems, pp. 437–446. ACM, April 2006
21. Xie, L., Antle, A.N., Motamedi, N.: Are tangibles more fun?: comparing children's enjoyment and engagement using physical, graphical and tangible user interfaces. In: Proceedings of the 2nd International Conference on Tangible and Embedded Interaction, pp. 191–198. ACM, February 2008

Innovating Media Usage

Question & Answering Interface to Improve the Students' Experience in an E-learning Course with a Virtual Tutor

João Balsa$^{(\boxtimes)}$ ⓘ, Luís Neves, Maria Beatriz Carmo ⓘ,
and Ana Paula Cláudio ⓘ

Biosystems & Integrative Sciences Institute (BioISI),
Faculdade de Ciências da Universidade de Lisboa, Lisbon, Portugal
jbalsa@ciencias.ulisboa.pt, fc51695@alunos.fc.ul.pt,
{mbcarmo,apclaudio}@fc.ul.pt

Abstract. E-learning courses offer, nowadays, opportunities for everyone to study wherever they are. However, asynchronous communication between students and teachers, and the lack of social engagement, leads frequently to a sense of abandonment and, in the limit, to withdrawal, as a consequence. To avoid this phenomenon, we developed an interface prototype with an anthropomorphic 3D virtual tutor in the Moodle's e-learning platform of Universidade Aberta (https://portal.uab.pt/). This virtual tutor helps students finding information in the page of the course, delivers speech, exhibits facial expressions and is able to answer questions about the course. This paper describes the approach used to implement this Q&A functionality. Having all the course information represented in an ontology, the idea is to transform the original question in a SPARQL query that, when executed on the defined ontology, returns the desired answer.

Keywords: Question & Answering · Virtual tutor · E-learning

1 Introduction

Nowadays, due to the widespread of internet communications, e-learning courses offer opportunities for everyone to study wherever they are. This may be especially relevant for adults longing for ameliorating their professional life. However, this educational approach introduces several challenges, such as, the asynchronous communication between students and teachers, and the lack of social engagement that is usual in the classical classroom teaching. Students' questions, even those that have a very urgent answer need, may not be instantaneously answered by the teacher or by their student peers. This may induce in the students a sense of abandonment, which increases significantly their effort to keep the motivation and leads frequently to withdrawal.

So, the existence of an online tutor 24 h/day, seems to be a valuable instrument to stimulate student's engagement and to work as an additional learning support tool. This is the main goal of our project, which involves an interface prototype with an

C. Sylla and I. Iurgel (Eds.): TIE 2019, LNICST 307, pp. 45–54, 2020.
https://doi.org/10.1007/978-3-030-40180-1_5

anthropomorphic 3D virtual tutor in the Moodle's e-learning platform of Universidade Aberta (Cláudio et al. 2018).

We explore in this contribution the possibility of allowing the user to ask the virtual tutor questions in natural language (Portuguese). This provides an easy way of finding information that might be "hidden" in the course webpage in the e-learning platform. We focus on questions regarding the course organization, but the methodology is adaptable to other topics. Having all the course information represented in an ontology, the idea is to transform the original question in a SPARQL query that, when executed on the defined ontology, returns the desired answer. A first version of this approach was already described in (Salgueiro et al. 2018). In this new version, two alternative evaluation methods are explored and compared.

2   State of the Art

The presence of virtual tutors in e-learning systems has positive effects in the learners' motivation and teaching effectiveness (Kokane et al. 2014). Several experiences have been made using virtual tutors in learning environments or support systems in the academic environment, ranging from 2D cartoon like virtual tutors (Maciel et al. 2014) to 3D realistic virtual humans (Currie et al. 2016; Kokane et al. 2014; Querrec et al. 2018) with diverse interaction and cognitive capabilities.

Kokane et al. (2014) developed an e-learning system (Learner Centered Design Approach of E-learning System) which integrates 3D virtual tutors to narrate to students summarized versions of the contents of the course. Together with the spoken narrative, the written text appears dynamically on the screen as the tutor speaks. Besides the help of the virtual tutors, the e-learning system provides the communication with human tutors through a real-time web-based video. Reports on the student activity and quiz results allow the human tutors to fine-tune the course contents. Maciel et al. (2014) also explored audio communication. They created a plug-in to the Moodle's e-learning platform within a HTML block that allows the automatic generation of audio and visemes for the virtual tutor. This solution enables the creation of the virtual tutor dialogues according to the current needs, for instance, message dissemination appropriate to the context. This work was later extended to enable notifications on mobile devices (Amaral et al. 2015). Silva et al. (2014) also worked with the Moodle platform, but they centered on the development of a multi-agent system to create an intelligent virtual tutor. Based on the analysis of the student's interaction with Moodle, their aim was to propose pedagogical interventions according to the needs and weaknesses of each student.

Providing intelligence to virtual assistants were also the focus of Currie et al. (2016). They developed a virtual assistant to guide students in university employability service through a text-to-speech interaction. A 3D virtual female answers students' questions in natural language communication in both text and speech. The Artificial Intelligence Markup Language (AIML) was used to interpret the rules for user interaction with the virtual assistant. Soliman and Guetl (2013) used as well AIML to implement a text-to-speech synthesis function for intelligent pedagogical agents. These virtual agents are inserted in a 3D virtual scenario where they can simulate experiments and give tutorials. The student interacts through text messages and the virtual agent answers either in voice or text together with gestures to express emotional support.

Question and Answering systems have seen a great growth in interest from companies that have web sites and, consequently, have been subject to a great demand for the development of innovative solutions. These systems use artificial intelligence techniques to present the user a response that is as accurate as possible, based on the question received. Some even striving to be as realistic as possible and developing conversations with the user as if it were a real person, giving more realistic answers and not repeating answers to the same question.

Despite this great growth, many systems still use fairly basic question and answer techniques, where, having a set of basic questions and corresponding answers, when a question is introduced by the user the most similar question is chosen to obtain the desired answer. The answer chosen is sometimes edited in order to maintain a more realistic conversation with the user. These systems do not have a highly developed artificial intelligence component, and the only thing that is needed is an algorithm to compare strings stored in a database.

Automatic question answering systems exist in a much lower number than the systems mentioned above, but there are some that present very promising results, although using ontologies in a different way than the one proposed in this article. Those systems use ontologies in order to improve the user's question, adding synonyms and more information to the question that will be sent to the web, improving the results obtained. Jayalakshmi and Sheshasaayee (2017), Mervin (2014) e Kwok et al. (2001) present work that have some similarities among them, where all of them use ontologies to improve user questions and make web queries more accurate.

To the best of our knowledge, there is no system developed that uses a similar methodology to the one presented in this paper.

3   Virtual Tutor in Moodle's Platform

Our prototype of the virtual tutor that was integrated in Moodle's platform of Universidade Aberta comprises two components: the interface for the student and the back-office for the teacher which provides a way to introduce information required to define the behavior of the virtual tutor in each specific course.

3.1   Virtual Tutor Interface

The virtual tutor interface for the student in a Moodle's course webpage contains an anthropomorphic representation, currently restricted to head and shoulders. The two 3D models of virtual tutors were produced by Didimo (http://www.mydidimo.com/) and are based on photographs of real people. The virtual tutor is implemented as a WebGL application inserted in the Moodle's course page within a HTML block. This application was developed using Unity3D and C# programming. The tutor is displayed inside a window that is superimposed over the Moodle's webpage of a curricular unit, it occupies a fixed position on the bottom right corner of the page, still allowing students to scroll up and down over this, as usual. The overall aspect of the interface in a

Moodle's page can be observed in Fig. 1. The tutor delivers speech (text, lips' movements, but no sound yet) and exhibits facial expressions.

Fig. 1. Virtual tutor's window in a Moodle's webpage.

Figure 2 displays the virtual tutor window. The text inside the balloon and the facial expression are coherent with the grades and assiduity of the student in the course, as explained ahead; the post-it lists the items in the webpage of the course with new information since the last login of the student and also remembers the utility of the six buttons at the bottom of the window, which provide information about the course. These buttons include a Q&A button and five buttons that provide direct access in the webpage to the plan of the curricular unit, and to the lists of: topics, forums, activities and e-folios (exercises that the student has to upload periodically and that are graded by the teacher). When one of these last buttons is pressed the interface uses colors to highlight the particular elements in these lists that are new since the last login of the student.

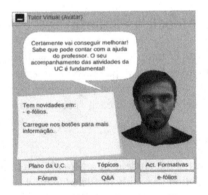

Fig. 2. Virtual tutor's window (in Portuguese)

According to the pedagogical model of the institution, shortly after the beginning of the semester, each student enrolled in a curricular unit has to choose among two evaluation modalities: continuous or final. The student in continuous modality is expected to solve and upload some e-folios periodically along the semester; these are graded by the teacher and, if these grades are above a particular mark, the student gets the right to do the final written exam (called p-folio). The alternative final modality implies only one written exam at the end of the semester.

The students evaluated in a continuous modality are the ones that could benefit the most from the virtual tutor in Moodle's curricular units, because they are expected to login regularly on the page and potentially need frequent synchronous support. Therefore, these students were identified as our target audience.

To provide a good support for the student, the behavior of the virtual tutor, which is expressed by facial expression and speech, has to be coherent with his/her performance and attitude in the curricular unit. To measure this, we define the state of the student, a value that depends on the following three values: (i) the evaluation, based on the grades obtained in the e-folios, (ii) the frequency of logins, and (iii) the number of messages the student posts in the forums of the course. The weighted combination of these two last values define the attendance of the student, used as a measure of participation in the course.

The teacher responsible for the course defines, in a back-office interface, two thresholds for each one of these three values. For instance, considering the evaluation, the teacher defines the minimal threshold that separates negative grades from positive ones, and a maximal threshold that separates average grades from very good grades.

Similarly, for the frequency of logins and the number of messages in the forums of the course, the teacher defines, for each one, a pair of thresholds and a weight that expresses its contribute to measure the attendance of the student.

As mentioned, the behavior of the virtual tutor is aligned with the performance and attitude of the student in the course measured by his/her state, but always in an empathic and supportive or rewarding way, never recriminatory. When a potential problematic situation is detected (for instance, a student with very low grades along the semester), the virtual tutor will exhibit a neutral expression while recommending and promoting the communication with the teacher of the course. But, if the student has very good grades and a good attendance value, the virtual tutor will show a smile and congratulates the student.

The facial expression is complemented by the speech in the balloon that also depends on the state of the student and always includes a component relative to the grades and a component relative to the attendance of the student. For the sake of variability, there are several phrases that are randomly combined.

3.2   Q&A Approach

The goal of the Q&A component is to provide an answer to the questions introduced by the student when she/he presses the corresponding button in the interface. To attain this, two separate modules are involved (see Fig. 3), one that processes the question and creates a SPARQL query, and the other that executes this query on an ontology and presents the resulting answer.

Fig. 3. Question Answering modules

The first step of the process is to find the sentence's grammatical dependencies. For this we used the Dependency Parser provided by the NLX Group (Reis and Branco 2006). In the current version, the system is able to answer questions regarding the course organization. Some possible questions in Portuguese are:

- Qual o código da UC de Análise Formal de Redes Sociais? (*What is the code for the Formal Analysis of Social Networks course?*)
- Qual é o significado de p-fólio? (*What is the meaning of p-folio?*)

The processing of each question by the parser creates a structure that expresses the dependencies between the words in the sentence. This structure comprises the following information:

- Form – the token
- Raw – the word as it appears in the text
- Lemma – the motto as for example "dictionary form"
- Pos – part-of-speech
- Infl – bending information (gender, number, time, aspect, etc.)
- Ne – named entity information (person, organization, etc.)
- Deprel – grammatical dependency relation (using the NLX tagset)
- Parent – token index that is the "head" of this token
- Udeprel - grammatical dependency relation (using the SUD (Stanford Universal Dependencies) tagset)
- Uparent – token index that is the "head" of this token using the SUD tagset

Figure 4 shows the dependency information obtained for the first question above. From the information in the "parent" and "uparent" fields, that provide information about which token is the "head" of the presented sentence, it's possible to visualize this structure as a dependency tree. Figure 5 represents the tree created by the previously sentence, using the NLX tagset. In this figure, we can observe a pattern that occurs in most of the tested questions. The first level corresponds to the verb of the sentence. The second level corresponds to the first word of the sentence and indicates the type of the question. In this case using the word "Qual" (*which*) we want a specific result to the question, but there are other cases that what is required is a value. For example, when the first word is "Quantos" (*How many*). This word is followed by the subject of the sentence which is one of the necessary expressions for the ontology query. Finally, the punctuation of the sentence appears, which in this case is a "?" because it is a question. The third level is an intermediate level that does not contain any information necessary to create the query.

In the fourth level we can observe that there is an important word for the query that is the object of the sentence, being present with a "deprel" of C or DO-ARG2 and being a child of the subject of the sentence. This object will be used in the query in conjunction with the other expression presented earlier.

form	raw	lemma	pos	infl	ne	deprel	parent	udeprel	uparent	space
Qual	Qual	_	INT	gs	O	SJ-ARG1	2	DEP	4	R
é	é	SER	V	pi-3s	O	ROOT	0	COP	4	LR
o	o	_	DA	ms	O	SP	4	DET	4	LR
código	código	CÓDIGO	CN	ms	O	PRD-ARG2	2	ROOT	0	LR
de_	de	_	PREP	_	I-ORG	OBL-ARG1	4	CASE	7	LR
a	_	_	DA	fs	I-ORG	SP	7	DET	7	R
UC	UC	_	PNM	_	I-ORG	C	5	POBJ	4	LR
de	de	_	PREP	_	I-ORG	N	7	MWE	7	LR
Análise	Análise	_	PNM	_	I-ORG	N	7	MWE	7	LR
Formal	Formal	_	PNM	_	I-ORG	N	7	MWE	7	LR
de	de	_	PREP	_	I-ORG	N	7	MWE	7	LR
Redes	Redes	_	PNM	_	I-ORG	N	7	MWE	7	LR
Sociais	Sociais	_	PNM	_	I-ORG	N	7	MWE	7	L
?	?	_	PNT	_	O	PUNCT	2	PUNCT	4	

Fig. 4. Information about a sentence obtained from the NLX Dependency Parser

```
| é
| Qual | código
|      | o | de
|          | UC
|          | a | de | Análise | Formal | de | Redes | Sociais |     | ? |
```

Fig. 5. Dependency tree created using the NLX tagset

Level five presents complementary information that can be used to improve information present in the ontology query. If any of the words present in this level have a "deprel" of N and is a child of the object, this indicates that it must be grouped with the predicate of the phrase because it is the continuation of this one. In the presented case the object would be "UC de Análise Formal de Redes Sociais".

The query to be sent to the ontology would then consist of the expression "code" (the predicate) and the expression "UC de Análise Formal de Redes Sociais".

There are some exceptions to note when there is no verb defined in the sentence, which changes the structure of the tree, passing the first word of the sentence that indicates the type of question, to the first level.

Other exceptions in which none of the cases mentioned above presents a valid result, is needed to make other comparisons using the "pos" column, where we can observe that the first expression necessary for the query is normally represented by "CN", and in the "ne" column we can confirm that the second expression is usually within the group that has the value other that "O" (Fig. 4).

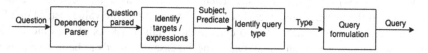

Fig. 6. Query creation process

Query Creation

The ultimate goal of this process is to create a SPARQL query in order to get, from the ontology, the answer to the user's question (Fig. 6). The main challenge is to find the components of the RDF triple that constitutes the query.

To cover all the questions, it was necessary to create six different types of queries:

1. Basic query following a standard pattern.
2. Definition query
3. Values query
4. Dates of components
5. SPARQL query with month filter
6. SPARQL query for UCs with month filter

The first three are domain independent queries, while the last three are domain dependent. Each query type corresponds to a different way of finding the relevant components in the result of the dependency parser. For instance, the first type corresponds to the creation of a basic query using the first and second expressions. For the case of the question "Qual o código da UC de Análise Formal de Redes Sociais?", mentioned earlier, the query would indicate which Individual (in this case "UC de Análise Formal de Redes Sociais") and then what Data Property ("código" in this case) will correspond to the "subject" and "predicate" of the query, being the answer obtained as the possible values for the "object" part of the triple. Figure 7 shows the query built for this question.

```
PREFIX rdf: <http://www.w3.org/1999/02/22-rdf-syntax-ns#>
PREFIX tv: <https://tutoria-virtual.uab.pt/>
SELECT ?a
WHERE {
              tv:UC_de_Análise_Formal_de_Redes_Sociais tv:código ?a
}
```

Fig. 7. Basic query for the question "Qual o código da UC de Análise Formal de Redes Sociais?"

Answering the question

The previously created query will be executed in an ontology, previously filled in, that contains all the information related to the course where the Virtual Tutor operates. When executing the query to the ontology it will return the result to the question asked by the user, if the query is correct, or a blank reply, otherwise.

With the response obtained it will be necessary to edit it in order to provide a response to the user that seems realistic. There are special cases that need to be edited, for example if the question indicates that the user wants a specific value instead of a list of the answers, it will be necessary to change the obtained values of the ontology so that the answer is a numerical value. Other special case that needs to be looked at is in case there are dates in the answer, where it will need to be formatted to an easier to read date format, since the format returned by the ontology is not commonly used.

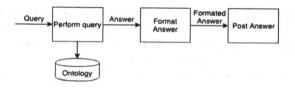

Fig. 8. Obtaining the answer

With these changes done it is finally necessary to make the responses more human, this is done using parts of the question asked by the user in order to construct a more complete answer (Fig. 8).

4   Evaluation and Discussion

In order to evaluate the methodology, a set of 1065 questions were processed. These questions were automatically created through a system which, using default questions and queries made to the ontology, creates questions similar to those a student may pose to the Q&A system. Additionally, some more specific questions were also entered manually.

Testing this method of obtaining expressions presented very good results. For the tests using the two tagsets, we can observe quite similar values between both methods, but concluding that the method using the NLX tagset was the one that presented the best results where in 48 of the sentences, the first expression was not obtained successfully and in the second expression it occurred 171 times. The value relative to the first expression occurs because the type of question to which it refers to, being a question of the type "O que significa ..." ("*What is the meaning of...*") and "O que é ..." ("*What is...*"). Of the 171 wrong expressions referring to the second expression necessary to perform the query to the ontology, 150 of these are due to an error in the categorization by the NLX Dependency Parser, where the system does not classify some names of the "Unidades Curriculares" as an expression, but rather as independent words, creating cuts in the expression. The remaining 21 expressions occur in the same sentences as those related to the errors presented in the first expression.

5   Conclusion

We presented a novel approach to improve the students' experience in e-learning contexts. The use of a graphically enhanced virtual tutor, capable of expressing emotions and able to answer questions posed in a natural language is an upgrade regarding previous work in this area. In what respects the question answering component, the results that were obtained from the presented project are quite good and within our expectations, only being found some failures in the response to the user and in cases where the question presents orthographic errors.

In the case of a query with a misspelling, the program will present errors, because the values that will be introduced in the ontology query will be different from the one in the ontology, thus causing the ontology results to be empty and the response returned to the user to be incorrect or empty. One way to solve this problem would be the use of dictionaries that allow you to store a set of keys and values, the keys being the words of a common dictionary and the values the definitions.

Regarding the failures presented in the user responses, they happen because it is necessary to find a better way of not giving a response to the user that seems automated, that is, the tutor responds in the same way to all the types of question not creating a conversation with the user.

Acknowledgements. This work was developed in the context of the FCT project PTDC/IVC-PEC/3963/2014 (proposed by Universidade Aberta). It is also supported by UID/MULTI/04046/2019 Research Unit grant from FCT, Portugal (to BioISI).

References

Amaral, Y., Maciel, A., Rodrigues, R.: Development of a virtual assistant for alerts and notifications in a learning environment. In: Brazilian Symposium on Computers in Education, vol. 26, p. 742 (2015)

Cláudio, A.P., et al.: Empathic mediators for distance learning courses. In: Proceedings International Conference on Graphics and Interaction, pp. 177–178 (2018)

Currie, E., et al.: An investigation into the efficacy of avatar-based systems for student advice. EAI Endorsed Trans. e-Learn. **e5**, 1–7 (2016). https://eudl.eu/issue/el/3/11

Jayalakshmi, S., Sheshasaayee, A.: Automated question answering system using ontology and semantic role. In: Proceedings of ICIMIA 2017, pp. 528–532 (2017)

Kokane, A., Singhal, H., Mukherjee, S., Reddy, G.R.M.: Effective E-learning using 3D virtual tutors and webRTC based multimedia chat. In: IEEE International Conference on Recent Trends in Information Technology (ICRTIT), pp. 1–6 (2014)

Kwok, C., Etzioni, O., Weld, D.S.: Scaling question answering to the web. ACM Trans. Inf. Syst. **19**(3), 242–262 (2001)

Maciel, A.M., Rodrigues, R.L., Carvalho, E.C.: Desenvolvimento de um assistente virtual integrado ao moodle para suporte a aprendizagem online. In: Brazilian Symposium on Computers in Education (Simpósio Brasileiro de Informática na Educação -SBIE), vol. 25, p. 382 (2014)

Mervin, R.: Knowledge based question answering system using ontology. Int. J. Eng. Sci. Res. Technol. **3**(10), 523–528 (2014)

Querrec, R., Taoum, J., Nakhal, B., Bevacqua, E.: Model for verbal interaction between an embodied tutor and a learner in virtual environments. In: International Conference on Intelligent Virtual Agents, 5–8 November, Sydney, NSW, Australia, 6 p. ACM, New York (2018)

Reis, R., Branco, A.: (2006). http://nlxserv.di.fc.ul.pt/depparser/intro_en.html

Salgueiro, A.M., Alves, C.B., Balsa, J.: Querying an ontology using natural language. In: Villavicencio, A., et al. (eds.) PROPOR 2018. LNCS (LNAI), vol. 11122, pp. 164–169. Springer, Cham (2018). https://doi.org/10.1007/978-3-319-99722-3_17

Silva, S.B., Machado, V.P., Araújo, F.N.: Sistema tutor inteligente baseado em agentes na plataforma moodle para apoio as atividades pedagógicas da universidade aberta do Piauí. In: Anais dos Workshops do Congresso Brasileiro de Informática na Educação, vol. 3, p. 592 (2014)

Soliman, M., Guetl, C.: Implementing intelligent pedagogical agents in virtual worlds: tutoring natural science experiments in OpenWonderland. In: Global Engineering Education Conference (EDUCON), pp. 782–789. IEEE (2013)

Exploring the Use of Augmented Reality Concepts to Enhance the TV Viewer Experience

Simão Carvalho[1], Teresa Romão[1(✉)], and Pedro Centieiro[1,2]

[1] NOVA LINCS, Faculdade de Ciências e Tecnologia,
Universidade NOVA de Lisboa, 2829-516 Caparica, Portugal
Spn.carvalho@campus.fct.unl.pt, tir@fct.unl.pt,
pcentieiro@gmail.com
[2] Viva Superstars Digital Media, Lda, Madan Parque, Rua Dos Inventores,
2825-182 Caparica, Portugal

Abstract. Television has no longer the same effect on viewers as it had decades ago. The time that was formerly spent watching "traditional" television is now shared with or replaced by mobile devices, such as smartphones and tablets. When using these devices, the viewer has the opportunity to further interact with the content that is provided to him, as well as with remote friends. The work presented in this paper explores new concepts of interaction in television contexts, which comprises the integration of augmented reality (AR) techniques with television shows to enhance the viewer's experience, allowing them to access additional information about the content they are watching and to create their own content to share with their friends. This paper describes the developed prototype and the corresponding preliminary user evaluation with promising results.

Keywords: Augmented reality · TV shows · Interaction with TV content · Social interaction · Mobile devices · Entertainment

1 Introduction

Once available to the world's population, television became an essential part of our daily routine. This technology can show us news from around the world and it can be a rich source of entertainment. This made television a main form of socializing, as well as a way to access information [1] until recently, when some changes in this scenario started to happen, as mobile devices started to gain ground against the TV, especially among young adults [2]. Younger generations are more familiar with interactive technology which provides them with the content they want at anyplace and at anytime. As smartphones and tablets can do the same as traditional television and much more, television is losing the audience it used to have among the younger generations.

Since its creation to the present day, television has undergone different evolutions to adapt to the new generations of viewers (such as the introduction of TV set boxes and IPTV). It is now possible to watch television over the Internet on a mobile device, and since it is estimated that more than 63% of world's population is in possession of a

© ICST Institute for Computer Sciences, Social Informatics and Telecommunications Engineering 2020
Published by Springer Nature Switzerland AG 2020. All Rights Reserved
C. Sylla and I. Iurgel (Eds.): TIE 2019, LNICST 307, pp. 55–64, 2020.
https://doi.org/10.1007/978-3-030-40180-1_6

mobile phone [3], television is on the verge of another major evolution. Like we use social networks to interact with multimedia content and to communicate and socialize with remote friends, we aim to bring the same kind of interactivity to the traditional passive experience of watching television.

This way, we seek to contribute to turn watching TV into a more interactive activity of entertainment and socialization. Thus, we have been exploring new forms of interaction with TV content that enhance the viewers' experience. To facilitate the viewers' access to additional information related with the TV show content they are watching, we explored the integration of Augmented Reality (AR) concepts with TV shows' content and developed tools for TV content edition and share. In this paper, we present our first concept, its realization as a prototype and results of usability tests which attempt to validate our approach and uproot design flaws.

2   Related Work

AR allows the user to observe the real world with superimposed virtual objects in a way that they seem to co-exist in the same space as real world objects. When we use AR, we intend to improve user's perception of and interaction with the real world [4], providing him with additional information about his surrounding world. From head-mounted display based to mobile applications, AR applications have been developed for a variety of areas, such as health [5], environmental management [6], education [7], tourism [8] and entertainment [9]. AR has also been used for real time augmentation of broadcast video, to enhance the visualization of sporting events and to place advertisements in the scene. An early example is the FoxTrax system, which tracks and highlights the location of a hockey puck as it moved rapidly across the ice [10]. In these situations, the end-viewer is not able to control the information he wants to visualize. There are already some studies in the area of mixing augmented reality with television broadcast, where the viewer can interact with the show he is watching. In [11], the authors propose a system that enables viewer-selectable augmented broadcasting services with the need for an extra device.

Interactive television combines traditional TV services with data services, allowing users' participation and feedback. It allows various forms of interaction, such as with TV-related content and TV services, delivered through specific pay-TV set-top boxes and controlled by extra devices, such as remote controls, mobile phones or tablets. Users may choose the viewing angle thanks to the existence of various cameras filming a match, participate in trivia quizzes along with other participants in the studio or at their own homes or check statistics. Olsen et al. [12] presents a system for interactive television news and the corresponding evaluation to understand interactive viewing behavior.

To provide the viewers with a more active role, we have been exploring how to create more interactive experiences, that allow them to control what they want to watch, when and where, as well as to access additional information and to create and share content based on the TV show they are watching. Thus, as explained next, we integrated AR techniques with video playback to complement the TV show content, and propose mechanisms for user social interaction that allows them to edit the video content they are watching and share the outcomes with their friends. Unlike, second screen applications for interaction with TV content [13], using our prototype the interaction is achieved through a unique mobile device (tablet or smartphone) that most users own and can carry wherever they want.

3 TvTeller: Prototype Description

We developed TvTeller prototype as a proof of concept which aims at exploring and changing the way people interact with the TV content they are watching. Using a mobile device as the screen for visualization and interaction, viewers are able to access additional information about the TV content they are watching, as well as to extract, edit and share video clips. This way, TvTeller provides users with the possibility to know more about TV series characters, create amusing content, and share it with their friends. As users, especially young people, often interact with their mobile devices to share content with friends and search for information, TvTeller explores how to non-intrusively integrate these activities within the experience of TV watching.

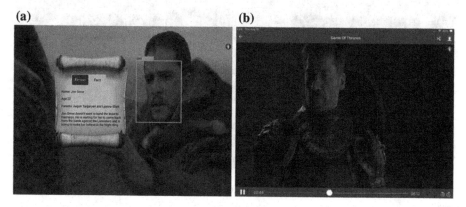

Fig. 1. While watching a TV series episode the user can click on a character to know more about him (a) when a character is identified for the first time and (b) when a character is recognized again later on (an icon "i" appears).

TvTeller is composed by two components that are independent from each other. One is more information-oriented and the other more entertainment-oriented. The first one allows the user to select a TV show episode and, while watching it, to know more about the characters or some other important elements, which may include animals and objects that appear on screen while the episode is played. While watching traditional television, when a user wants to know more about what he is watching, he needs to search for it outside the TV context (for example, using his mobile phone to search the Internet), diverting his attention from the TV show. Using TvTeller, the TV series is augmented with virtual information objects superimposed on the video which provide additional information regarding the elements of the displayed scene (Fig. 1a). The user does not need to move his eyes from the screen to obtain information on a new TV series he just started to follow or recall details from a TV series former season. Instead of superimposing virtual objects on the video coming from a camera, as in "traditional" mobile AR systems, we superimpose the virtual objects directly on the video itself.

The entertainment-oriented component allows users to trim parts of an episode, creating short video clips that can be edited and shared later on. This is a non-intrusive task, as the viewer can trim a moment that he liked while he continues to watch the episode (as explained in Sect. 3.1). After the trim is done, the user can edit the trimmed video adding virtual objects to the characters that appear in it (Fig. 2) and share the creations with others. Since sharing funny content is something very usual nowadays (e.g. meme photos and videos), we intend to facilitate this task and enhance the user's motivation to watch the episode with more attention, as he can find and record the perfect moment(s) of the episode to share.

(a)   (b)

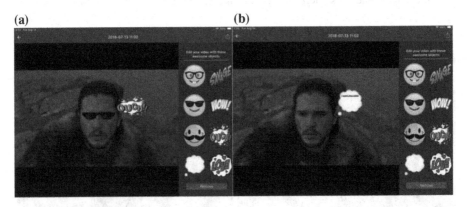

Fig. 2. Gallery editor view: (a) adding virtual objects to a character and (b) adding a bubble object.

Although this concept may be applied to any TV series or show, the series "Game of Thrones" was used as the case study. This series, due to its popularity and its unique characteristics, is a good example to demonstrate our concept. For example, it has a lot of characters, so it is easy to forget who someone is and whether he did something that changed the course of the plot. Besides, it is a show with some recasts, which can confuse a viewer when he sees a new actor for the first time playing an existing role. Our concept can also be used in movies (especially when they have sequels), as well as with almost every TV content, such as reality shows, sitcoms, or documentaries.

3.1 Interaction

In the TvTeller main screen, the user can choose from watching a TV series episode or go to the gallery where he can find the clips that he has saved earlier.

When the user selects to watch an episode, he is presented with a grid view of the available series from which he can select the one he wants to watch. After selecting an episode, the video starts playing and the user can activate the recognition feature, touching on the face button on the top right of the screen in the navigation bar (Fig. 1b). When this feature is activated, the faces of the characters on the screen are recognized and a rectangular bounding box appears around them when a character is identified for the first time (Fig. 1a). The following times, only an icon "i" appears on the top right of the screen, in a less intrusive way (Fig. 1b). The user can touch on the character to visualize information about the character/actor. It is also possible to access information about non-human characters or objects. Since these elements have no face, to inform the user that he can access more information about the character or the object, an icon "i" also appears on the top right of the screen.

Besides accessing information regarding the elements on the screen while watching a series, when the user likes a specific moment of the episode, he can trim that moment of the video which is saved in the gallery for later edition and sharing. In order to facilitate this task (video trimming), the user only has to touch on the trim button, which looks like a scissor, when he watches the moment he wants to save. 15 s of the video are recorded: 13 s before the button touch (as the user decides to trim the video after he visualized the moment) and 2 s after (preventing the desired clip to end abruptly). We chose this duration because this kind of clips should be kept short and, according to our experiments, in most situations, this duration is appropriate to capture the relevant content the user wants to record.

In the gallery, the user can find all the moments he saved while watching his series. Selecting one of these moments (video clip), opens it in the editor view (Fig. 2). Here, the user is able to choose one of the available virtual objects to superimpose on the characters and change their appearance. There are two types of objects: face objects and bubble objects. Face objects, such as moustaches or glasses, are automatically super-imposed on characters' faces, adjusting to the face layout. Bubble objects, such as thought balloons, are placed, by the user, near the face of a specific character. After the user drags the thought balloon image close to a character face, he touches on it to bound the object to the face. The pre-defined bubble objects appear near the selected face for 1.5 s (Fig. 2b). In the empty thought balloon, the user needs to write the text to be displayed. This balloon appears for 3 s instead of 1.5 s, to give the users time to read the information in it. After adding an object, the user can remove the objects if he does not like them, add more objects, save the video in the gallery or share his creation.

3.2 Implementation and Architecture Workflow

Three main algorithms were developed to enable the TvTeller operation (Fig. 3).

To avoid performance issues from deteriorating the user experience while watching a TV show, each TV show episode must be pre-processed before it is ready to be watched. The facial and object recognition algorithm (1) receives the TV show file as the input and returns a JSON file containing the characters' faces and objects that appear in the frames of the video. Every 0.4 s (achieved by experimental observation), a frame of the video is analyzed and faces and objects are recognized. When recognition is achieved with more than 80% confidence, the identity of the face (or object), its location on the frame and the time of the frame are stored. This information, stored in the output JSON file, is used to provide the user with the augmented information about the characters and objects while he is watching the TV show, giving him the impression that it is made in real time. Detection and recognition are done using algorithms from Apple's Vision framework [14]. Apple has already some machine learning models to identify a variety of objects, but since we need some very specific models, we had to create them ourselves, using Tensorflow [15]. Another JSON file that contains the information about the characters and works as a dictionary, linking the ids of the recognized characters with the corresponding information, is part of our bundle resources. When the user taps the screen to watch additional information about a recognized character or special element, a function fetches this information from the dictionary.

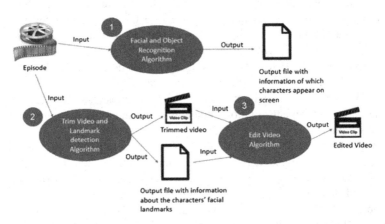

Fig. 3. Algorithms used in TvTeller.

To allow users to augment the video clips they have trimmed and stored in the gallery with virtual objects that must be registered over the characters' faces (face objects), an algorithm for face landmark detection (2) was developed. This algorithm detects the facial landmarks of every character that appears on the trimmed video and runs right when the user clicks to trim the video while watching an episode. First, the video is trimmed and saved inside the app's document directory. After that, a function runs the landmark detection algorithm and produces a JSON file containing the landmarks positions. We need to know with a good precision where are the landmarks located, so we can precisely superimpose objects on top of a face or near it. The augmented objects need to move with the character as smoothly as possible along the video clips, so the ideal was to gather information related to all frames of the trimmed video. However, this was time-consuming, so after some experimentation, we confirmed that analyzing a frame every 0.1 s provides sufficient information to achieve an appropriate dynamic registration of the augmented objects along the whole video in a suitable time period.

The edit video algorithm (3) is responsible for overlaying the selected virtual objects to all the frames in a trimmed clip stored in the gallery that is being edited and for the creation of the new video that can be shared. This algorithm uses the output file generated by the landmark detection algorithm (2) described before. After the user places an object on the clip being edited, the algorithm starts by identifying the nearest face in the frame. Then, it checks the position of the face in the next frame 0.1 s latter (this is done to move the virtual object smoothly between frames, in order to follow the face). If the face is near the same position, then the algorithm starts using the new position to check for the position of the face in the following frame (also in the next 0.1 s), otherwise (or if the face is not detected during 0.5 s) the virtual object is removed. This process goes on until the face disappears or for the maximum time an object is kept on the clip.

4   Evaluation

After developing the TvTeller prototype, user tests were performed to evaluate its usability, test our concept and to gather feedback regarding how the application was going to be used, so we could fix some flaws and make it more user friendly.

4.1   Participants and Methodology

Users tests were conducted with a total of 30 users (22 were male and 8 were female) with ages between 14 and 53 years old ($\bar{x} = 26,7$). All tests were made using the same device, an iPad Air 2. Before starting the tests, the users were provided with a brief explanation of the TvTeller concept, and during the tests, we observed the behaviour of the participants, took notes, and provided assistance if anyone had a problem. The participants were provided with a list of tasks to execute, available on a computer, but they were free to use the prototype as they liked. The tasks included watching an episode from Game of Thrones, turning character recognition on and visualizing augmented information about characters, actors and objects, trimming a moment of the episode, editing the trimmed video clip adding a bubble object, and sharing the resulting clip on a social network. After the test, the users filled in a questionnaire.

4.2   Results and Discussion

The questionnaire focused on usability and user experience issues, including general feedback about the TvTeller, its usability and ease of use. The first section included participants' personal data, such as age and genre. The second section contained questions about their habits while watching TV series. Half of the participants (50%) watch series on a daily basis, 13.3% watch almost every day, 30% watch series on a weekly basis (some users stated that this is due to the series they watch only released one episode per week) and 6.7% rarely watch TV series. The most used devices to watch TV series are: the computer selected by 83.3% of the participants, television (70%), smartphone (36.7%) and tablets (6.7%). Finally, 90% of the participants stated they use to watch meme videos, meaning that they were familiar with the theme.

The third section concerns how easy it was to perform the main available tasks. The users were asked to rate statements, using a five-point Likert-type scale, which ranged from "Very hard" (1) to "Very easy" (5). Table 1 shows that most of the tasks were considered very easy to perform by most of the users (S1–S3, S5). Adding objects to the trimmed video on the gallery was not so easy, as users were trying to understand how the face and bubble objects worked (S4). Some suggested to change the face objects' images, because the ones used give the impression that not only a moustache or glasses will be added over the characters' face, but the whole smiley image.

Table 1. Summary of the questionnaire results (third section). Higher scores are highlighted.

Statements	Very Hard	Hard	Neutral	Easy	Very Easy
S1. Activate facial recognition	0%	0%	10%	16.7%	73.33%
S2. Extract a clip from the video	0%	0%	3.33%	30%	66.67%
S3. Visualize info about the characters	0%	0%	0%	30%	70%
S4. Add objects to trimmed video clips	0%	3.3%	6.67%	46.67%	43.33%
S5. Share the clip on a social network	0%	0%	0%	13.33%	86.67%

The fourth section focuses on usability and entertainment aspects. In this section, the users were asked to rate statements, using a five-point Likert-type scale, which ranged from "Strongly Disagree" (1) to "Strongly Agree" (5), as presented in Table 2. All users considered the augmented information about the characters useful and complementary for their experience (S6). The characters' facial recognition bounding box (Fig. 1a) did not disturb the experience of most users, but a few users complained (S7). Most users were able to trim video clips without losing their focus on the series they were watching (S8), and they stated they would use the facial recognition feature in a real-life context (S9). While a few users were not interested in creating new video content (S10), most users said they would react to content shared by others (S11) and considered they could have fun watching that content (S12). Users also stated that TvTeller may help them to catch up on a series they have not follow for a while or may help them to follow an episode when they are performing another task while watching it. Observation of the users while testing the prototype corroborates with these results.

Table 2. Summary of the questionnaire results (fourth section). Higher scores are highlighted.

Statements	Strongly Disagree	Disagree	Neutral	Agree	Strongly Agree
S6. Additional information about the characters is useful and complemented my experience	0%	0%	0%	30%	70%
S7. The appearance of the facial recognition box did not disturb my experience	6.67%	3.33%	10%	43.33%	36.67%
S8. I can easily extract a video clip without losing focus on the series I am watching	0%	6.67%	13.33%	30%	50%
S9. In a real context, I would use facial recognition functionality while watching my series	0%	6.67%	23.33%	30%	40%
S10. Probably, I will create content to share	3.33%	13.33%	23.33%	33.33%	26.67%
S11. Probably, I will react to content created by others	0%	0%	16.67%	46.67%	36.67%
S12. Even if I do not watch a show, I can entertain myself with content that others created	0%	3.33%	13.33%	33.33%	50%

5 Conclusions and Future Work

With this work we aimed at exploring the possibility of turning the experience of watching a TV show into a more active and social one, allowing users to non-intrusively perform tasks they usually carry out while watching TV, such as search for information or share content with friends. In order to evaluate our concept, we created a prototype that gives the users the possibility to know more about their favorite series resorting to facial recognition and the opportunity to create new content to share with friends using augmented reality concepts.

In general, users liked the features presented in this prototype and the possibility of effortlessly perform additional tasks that do not disturb their focus on the TV content. Adding objects to a face, such as the moustache, is something that they are already used to, using face filters on applications like Instagram or Snapchat, and they loved the possibility to add them to TV characters. The feature that allows users to visualize information about the characters was also very well received. Some users stated that this feature solves some of their problems while watching a TV series, since they had the necessity to know more about the characters while they were watching TV series. Most of the users were able to perform the tasks without losing their focus on the TV content, however improvements can still (and will) me made.

In the future, we aim to solve some problems reported by users, regarding the UI and the facial detection algorithm. We also aim to take this concept even further and identify the facial expression of the characters to create new animations based on emotions, add sound clips or change the characters' faces instead of only adding objects to them.

Acknowledgments. This work is funded by FCT/MCTES NOVA LINCS PEst UID/CEC/ 04516/2019.

References

1. Gerbner, G., Gross, L., Morgan, M., Signorielli, N.: Living with television: the dynamics of the cultivation process. In: Bryant, J., Zillman, D. (eds.) Perspectives on Media Effects, pp. 17–40. Lawrence Erlbaum, New Jersey (1986)
2. Richter, F.: Smartphones beat Tv for young adults in the U.S, Statista (2017). https://www.statista.com/chart/8660/smartphone-vs-tv-usage/. Accessed 20 June 2019
3. Statista.: Number of mobile phone users worldwide from 2013 to 2019 (in billions). https://www.statista.com/statistics/274774/fore-cast-of-mobile-phone-users-worldwide/. Accessed 20 June 2019
4. Azuma, R., Baillot, Y., Behringer, R., Feiner, S., Julier, S., MacIntyre, B.: Recent advances in augmented reality. IEEE Comput. Graph. Appl. **21**(6), 34–47 (2001)
5. Bernhardt, S., Nicolau, S.A., Soler, L., Doignon, C.: The status of augmented reality in laparoscopic surgery as of 2016. Med. Image Anal. **37**, 66–90 (2017)
6. Romão, T., et al.: ANTS – augmented environments. Comput. Graph. **28**(5), 625–633 (2004)
7. Billinghurst, M., Kato, H., Poupyrev, I.: The MagicBook: a transitional AR interface. Comput. Graph. **25**(5), 745–753 (2001)
8. Střelák, D., Škola, F., Liarokapis, F.: Examining user experiences in a mobile augmented reality tourist guide. In: Proceedings of the 9th ACM International Conference on PErvasive Technologies Related to Assistive Environments (PETRA 2016), Corfu, Greece, 29 June–01 July. ACM New, York (2016)
9. Lv, Z., Halawani, A., Feng, S., Ur Réhman, S., Li, H.: Touch-less interactive augmented reality game on vision-based wearable device. Pers. Ubiquit. Comput. **19**(3–4), 551–567 (2015)
10. Cavallaro, R.: The FoxTrax hockey puck tracking system. IEEE Comput. Graph. Appl. **17**(2), 6–12 (1997)
11. Kim, S.C., Koo, H.S., Kim, H., Cheong, J.: Implementation of AR-based hybrid broadcasting system by TV viewer's preferred content provider. In: Proceedings of Information Science and Security (ICISS 2016), Pattaya, Thailand, 19–22 December. IEEE (2016)
12. Olsen, D.R., Sellers, B., Boulter, T.: Enhancing interactive television news. In: Proceedings of TVX 2014, Newcastle, UK, 25–17 June. ACM, New York (2014)
13. Centieiro, P., Cardoso, B., Romão, T., Dias, A.E.: If you can feel it, you can share it! A system for sharing emotions during live sports broadcasts. In: Proceedings of ACE 2014, Funchal, Portugal, 11–14 November. ACM, New York (2014)
14. Apple Vision framework: https://developer.apple.com/documentation/vision. Accessed 06 Feb 2019
15. Tensorflow: https://www.tensorflow.org/. Accessed 06 Apr 2019

Design Experiments in Nonrepresentational VR and Symmetric Texture Generation in Real-Time

Nikitas M. Sgouros[✉]

Department of Digital Systems, University of Piraeus, 18534 Piraeus, Greece
sgouros@unipi.gr

Abstract. Nonrepresentational VR environments present enormous opportunities for offering novel perceptual experiences, but their design can be significantly challenging due to the lack of appropriate tools and methodologies that can aid the designer compared to their representational counterparts. We describe our experience in developing Quoternion and Atypical, two nonrepresentational mobile VR apps focused on exploring a non-objective virtual space. We highlight and justify our design choices and report preliminary results on their efficacy. Furthermore, we describe Symmetricom, our Android app that allows designers to experiment with animated texture design based on the application of plane symmetry groups on real-time camera input and projected on various type of surfaces. All our systems are free and available for public use.

Keywords: Mobile VR · Nonrepresentational design · Geometric design · Symmetry · Creativity

1 Design Experiments in Nonrepresentational VR

Although virtual reality environments provide endless opportunities for novel perceptual experiences, many applications in this area restrict themselves to representational iconography and goal-directed activities (e.g., battles/fights, races, games, training simulations etc.). The design of such representational environments is based on the development of models (objects or processes) that simulate to a degree the real world. Nonrepresentational iconography refers to the depiction of objects and spaces that do not represent real objects. Opportunistic interaction refers to the embedding of the user in situations that present opportunities to act and explore a virtual environment rather than being subservient to specific goals imposed by the system. In nonrepresentational and opportunistic VR the lack of correspondence between perceptual and real-world experiences can be a mixed blessing. On the one hand, infinite design opportunities emerge as the analogs of real-world constraints can be ignored. On the other hand, this can lead to incomprehensible or alienating experiences. At the same time nonrepresentational design as a process is more complex due to the sparsity of tools and methods that can aid the designer in such systems.

We describe our experience with the development of two nonrepresentational mobile VR systems, Quoternion [8] and Atypical [9]. Quoternion is a minimal game in

C. Sylla and I. Iurgel (Eds.): TIE 2019, LNICST 307, pp. 65–70, 2020.
https://doi.org/10.1007/978-3-030-40180-1_7

which the user navigates a non-objective space seeking to drive a set of spheres in a designated area in the presence of another distinct set of moving spherical objects that can collide with and deflect the user-controlled spheres. The environment imposes no time limits and there is no scoring, thus allowing the user to freely explore a constantly varying non-objective visual backdrop, while listening to philosophical quotes from a computer-generated voice and improvisatory jazz samples (see [7] for a short video of the work). Atypical is a variation on the same visual theme as Quotemion differing in that the user position remains fixed and there is no game played. Instead the user can probe the environment by firing spherical objects at desired directions. If these objects collide with other moving objects a random audio, video or textual effect is created. Furthermore, in Atypical the environment constantly provides interaction opportunities through the generation of novel biomorphic objects consisting of flower textures projected in constantly changing geometries and various other moving shapes. The difference in user position between these two systems reflects our desire for Quotemion to be used by a user standing up and able to freely rotate, while Atypical can be used while sitting. Since there are no real-life analogs to base one's creative efforts, non-representational VR design has to rework the basics of form, color, motion, rhythm and sound to this new medium. In this respect, it faces similar problems to those negotiated by early 20th century abstract artists such as Kandinsky [5] or Mondrian [6]. In addition, we believe that the absence of real-life grounding of the experience motivates the user to actively construct meaning based on his personal experiences similar to what is the case in non-objective art [4]. Based on these observations, we strove for a completely stochastic and geometrical visual backdrop for our environments. This consists of a varying set of spheres and cubes that are continuously deformed and rotated with different speeds. In addition each such surface is rendered using two rotating texture coordinate systems over which continuously deforming star and circle shapes with varying colors are mapped. There is no correlation between the transformations applied to the objects forming the visual backdrop. Consequently, the user feels that there is no coordinated motion of the backdrop objects, something that we have found empirically to reduce the appearance of vection. Furthermore, the space is populated with rigid moving spheres with stable color patterns. These spheres offer interaction opportunities to the user. All moving objects use periodic functions in their transformation thus allowing the imposition of a desired rhythm in their individual behavior. Rhythm is also imposed by the use of a constant rhythmic part (a drum loop in the case of Quotemion a piano waltz in the case of Atypical) embellished with jazz samples for Quotemion or random piano or percussive samples notes for Atypical that are triggered by user actions in the environment. In both cases we impose no restrictions on the ways with which the user interacts with the environment. In Quotemion the game is presented as an opportunity to enrich the exploratory experience rather than a task, while in Atypical the user can choose whether to probe the environment or not. Consequently, she has total freedom to explore each environment at her leisure. Furthermore, in Quotemion the user decides whether to move or stop by pressing a controller button. The direction of motion is always forward from the current orientation of the user's head. Therefore the user's motion is always deliberate and predictable providing a consistent kinesthetic experience. Figure 1 gives an idea of the overall visual environment in these environments. Our preliminary trials with ten users

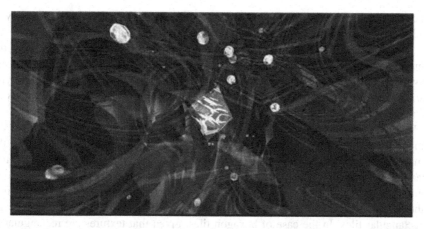

Fig. 1. Example of nonrepresentational visual backdrop and moving objects in Quoternion.

indicate that they find this interaction pleasing. We have observed no adverse reactions (e.g., nausea) so far for uses of the system averaging 20 min.

On a more practical level we envision the use of Quoternion and Atypical as parallel supporting activities that can maintain engagement in a boring or unpleasant main task and enrich the overall experience. For example, we have started testing Quoternion and Atypical while exercising on a treadmill or indoor bicycle with encouraging results. We will try to test both systems in more somber environments related to patients undertaking chemotherapy or hemodialysis treatments.

2 Symmetrical Texture Generation in Real-Time

Symmetrical patterns have been a constant source of inspiration for various visual art forms by evoking feelings of order, harmony or balance [1]. Furthermore, the existence of detailed mathematical descriptions for generating all possible symmetries on the plane has opened up the possibility of efficient, algorithmic generation of such patterns. The kinds of iconography that can be generated from symmetry is vast and can be made even bigger by combining symmetrical forms with color or motion animation or by introducing noise in such patterns in a principled way. In this case, the important question that concerns us is how we can efficiently help and motivate digital artists to create and experiment with symmetrical designs that are visually interesting and aesthetically pleasing. Our efforts in dealing with this question focus on the creation of digital environments for creative visual exploration of symmetrical patterns and their interplay with geometry and animation. We want to create tools that can be easily deployed by artists and designers, therefore we target mobile devices as our main development platform. To this end we have created and deployed Symmetricon [10], a free app for generating, animating and displaying, in real-time, plane symmetry patterns. Symmetricon is able to create 30 types of plane symmetries [3] from either the camera stream, or images and videos stored in a mobile device. There exist a variety of mobile apps that focus on the generation of symmetrical patterns (e.g. Kaleidoscope Pro, Picasso, etc.). Most of them are drawing apps that allow the user to create the primary cell and then generate mainly kaleidoscope tessellations. To the best of our knowledge Symmetricon is the only existing app that can generate animated, symmetrical tessellations from real-time camera stream and apply them as textures to various surfaces.

The symmetrical texture generation process in Symmetricon receives as input the frames captured from the camera stream of a mobile phone. These frames comprise the primary cells for the subsequent operations. Symmetricon then generates the final repeating tile which is either a rectangle or a hexagon depending on the symmetry group specified by the user. This tile is a bitmap image which is passed as a texture unit to the fragment shader of an OpenGL environment. This is straightforward in the case of rectangular tiles. In the case of hexagon tiles, given that textures are rectangular in OpenGL, the hexagon tile is turned into a rectangle by adding the top left triangle to the bottom right side of the hexagon and so on. The rest of the operations consisting of all the motions (translations, rotations, reflections and glides) applied to the repeating cell in order to create the tessellation are being performed in the fragment shader in parallel thus speeding the tessellating process and achieving real-time performance. In parallel with the generation of the tessellation the fragment shader computes the animation pattern specified by the user in the GPU as well. This can either be a horizontal/vertical translation of adjacent rows/columns of the tessellation, a rotation of a 4×4 tile block around its geometrical center or non-linear vortex and tunnel effects. The resulting tessellation is being pasted upon either a square surface, a sphere surface, a square grid (a square surface sampled with a grid of points) or a combination of the above depending on the user choice. The user can select a variety of animations thus creating various wave and geometrical deformation special effects. Symmetricon allows the user to select the types of symmetry groups he wants to use, the size of the tessellation along with the specific texturing surface (square, sphere or rugged plane) he wants to create and the type of animation he wants to employ on the pattern (none, horizontal, vertical, cyclical, vanishing, tunnel or pulsating effects). Based on these user specifications, the system creates a tessellation of the desired symmetrical pattern and embeds the resulting texture in a 3D scene. The user can then view the generated texture from any distance or viewing angle in this 3D space. He can also store the textures he finds interesting as images in his phone. Symmetricon provides the designer with the opportunity to generate and test various motifs under an unlimited set of continuous and constantly changing imaging conditions. This enables the app to be used as a visual exploration environment that allows its users to create infinite color and geometrical variations of symmetrical textures using as raw material real-world scenes captured by the camera of a mobile device. In this case, the artist/designer can control the camera position and motion of the mobile device during the capturing of the raw material while also applying on it various animation patterns and projecting it on various surfaces. A video showing a selection of patterns created by an extended version of Symmetricon while randomly scanning a typical office space with the camera of the mobile device can be found in [2]. The particular app version used in the video is able to project the textures simultaneously on an unlimited set of texturing surfaces where each

  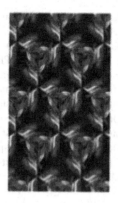

Fig. 2. Three examples of tessellations generated by Symmetricon.

of these surfaces is specified by the user. Figure 2 provides some more examples of the possible tessellations created with Symmetricon.

3   Conclusions and Future Work

Our goal is to create systems for the design and exploration of nonrepresentational environments that can be easily deployed and used. This is the reason we base our development efforts on mobile platforms. Quoternion and Atypical run on the Daydream platform while Symmetricon is available for Android phones. Our future research efforts in the case of Quoternion and Atypical will focus on the enrichment of their iconography and interaction opportunities. In the case of Symmetricon we will focus on speeding up further the tessellation process by parallelizing the primary cell generation which currently is executed on the CPU. Finally, we are developing synthesis environments for nonrepresentational graphics that can fully exploit multi-core processor architectures. In this case we create process grids, where each process corresponds to a pixel with full messaging capabilities between then to explore the dynamic generation of nonobjective patterns, their interactions and the iconography they produce.

Acknowledgments. Presentation of this paper was partially supported by the University of Piraeus Research Center.

References

1. Kappraff, J.: Connections: The Geometric Bridge between Art and Science, 2nd edn. World Scientific, Singapore (1991)
2. https://www.youtube.com/watch?v=TLYrzXQsg4k
3. Schattschneider, D.: The plane symmetry groups: their recognition and notation. Am. Math. Mon. **85**(6), 439–450 (1978)

4. Kandel, E.: Reductionism in Art and Brain Science. Columbia University Press, New York (2016)
5. Kandinsky, W.: Point and Line to Plane. Dover, Illinois (1926)
6. Tosaki, E.: Mondrian's Philosophy of Visual Rhythm - Phenomenology, Wittgenstein, and Eastern thought. Springer, Netherlands (2017). https://doi.org/10.1007/978-94-024-1198-0
7. https://www.youtube.com/watch?v=eIjpRCfTo-U
8. https://play.google.com/store/apps/details?id=org.epinoetic.hyperreal&pcampaignid=MKT-Other-global-all-co-prtnr-py-PartBadge-Mar2515-1
9. https://play.google.com/store/apps/details?id=org.epinoetic.atypical&pcampaignid=MKT-Other-global-all-co-prtnr-py-PartBadge-Mar2515-1
10. https://play.google.com/store/apps/details?id=org.epinoetic.symmetricon&pcampaignid=MKT-Other-global-all-co-prtnr-py-PartBadge-Mar2515-1

Innovation for Special Needs

Didactic Toy for Children with Special Needs

João Salgado[1], Filomena Soares[2(✉)] (iD), and Vítor Carvalho[3] (iD)

[1] Department of Industrial Electronics, University of Minho,
Guimarães, Portugal
a68529@alunos.uminho.pt
[2] Department of Industrial Electronics, R&D Centre Algoritmi,
University of Minho, Guimarães, Portugal
fsoares@dei.uminho.pt
[3] 2Ai - Technology School, Polytechnic Institute of Cavado and Ave,
Barcelos, Portugal
vcarvalho@ipca.pt

Abstract. In the last years, technology is receiving an important role in the development of new games and toys for children with special needs. In this paper a configurable prototype game is presented specially designed for children with special needs. The goal is to promote reaction and memory skills as well cooperative work in these children. The toy is capable of producing audio and visual sensations and it has more than one playable game (a reaction game, a memory game and a multiplayer game). Furthermore, it is an important tool for the therapists, since all gaming plays are tracked and registered in a database to posteriorly being filtered and presented using statistic methodologies. Preliminary tests were performed in real environment with children mainly with cerebral palsy. The feedback is promising enough to take it to the next step, which will be the integration of artificial intelligence approaches.

Keywords: Serious game · Adapted toy · Inclusive technology

1   Introduction

Play is a right of every children. This simple action has even more importance in the early ages, when children acquire basic skills [1]. In children with special needs, besides all the different impairments, there are some competencies that are not developed in early stages but can be stimulated while playing an adapted toy. Following this idea, the action of play gains an extra importance as it may help children to promote their skills, overcoming their impairments, in a pleasant environment [2, 3]. Also, therapists lack tools to automatically register and analyze the evaluation of their patients, being restricted to their experience and direct behavior observation [4].

Even though the technology advance, the inclusive toys are not going along. The few ones available hardly keep the children focused for a long time, becoming boring and monotonous. The solutions found are now restricted to the digital world and the toys are substituted by the electronic devices [5–8].

The goal of this work is to design and develop a configurable game play for children with special needs that promotes reaction and memory skills as well

C. Sylla and I. Iurgel (Eds.): TIE 2019, LNICST 307, pp. 73–79, 2020.
https://doi.org/10.1007/978-3-030-40180-1_8

cooperative work. The first steps of this on-going work were the proof of concept of the game. Further actions are taken in order to include adaptation in the game based on child actions and performance.

This paper is organized in four sections. Section 2 presents the toy development, Sect. 3 shows the preliminary tests and results obtained and the last Sect. 4 addresses the conclusions and future considerations.

2   Toy Development

In order to achieve a versatile solution there were developed three different games. The type of activities, the game configuration, and user interaction were defined in collaboration with the therapists that accompany the children. This first prototype took in account the therapists' needs in their intervention sessions.

The modes of the gamepad are automatically remapped to the buttons which are randomized for every new game. The game includes a Backoffice interface for the therapists to observe the children evolution in the games.

The first game is called the reaction game. It was developed in order to the players test their reaction and audio memory. The game occurs in a loop mode limited by the number of plays. When a button is activated a timer is initiated, and the player must press it as fast as he/she can. The timer stops and the time spent is saved in a file.

The second game is focused on memory training and rapid response. There is a random sequence of active buttons and the players must press the buttons in the same sequence. If the players get it right, the next sequence will be faster and if he/she fails, it will be slower. Also, the play times are saved.

The third is a multiplayer game. The board is divided in two identical parts for each player. In the left part one presses the button and the other player must press the symmetric one. The player who press the buttons faster wins.

2.1   Toy Design

The toy gamepad was created in a way to provide a visual sensation capable to arouse the interest of the children. As shown in Fig. 1, this consists of ten light buttons: one small white, one small blue, two small green, two small red, two big blue and two big yellow.

All of them are used in the games except the white button that only needs to be pressed to restart the game. Each button is integrated with a LED, which is respectively associated in the processor. The button disposition was designed in a way to call for the children's attention and to provide difficulty levels by having the small ones in a second line.

2.2 Game Architecture

The game is controlled by an ATMega328p microcontroller that executes all the tasks [9], mainly the activation or deactivation of a LED, button information capture, trigger or stop a sound, and read or write in the SD Card. The card is located on the right side of the game box, and it stores the player identification and performance in each gameplay for further analysis by the therapist.

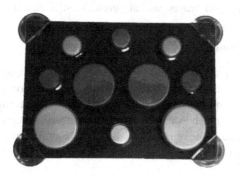

Fig. 1. Toy gamepad (Color figure online)

In Fig. 2 is the block diagram of the game architecture.

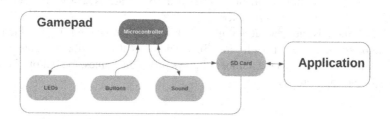

Fig. 2. Game architecture

2.3 Gamepad Images

An alternative to the gameplay is to have images and sound instead of sequences of light buttons. The available categories are animals, musical instruments and numbers. The therapist place the images on the buttons (Fig. 3). When the game starts, a sound of an onomatopoeia, a musical instrument or a number is activated and the child must press the corresponding button. The system may be configured to have other categories.

Fig. 3. Gamepad images: animals, musical instruments and numbers.

2.4   Games Development

The game development was based on C++ language and is implemented in the micro controller. First, the toy has a menu function, where all the information about settings is processed. The player must enter his/her identification by pressing four buttons that represent four digits. After, he/she chooses the game that is represented on the three activated buttons and each one represents a different game. When the game finishes, the player has the option to play it again by pressing the white button.

2.5   Interface Application

The application was developed using the QT Platform using the program language C++. It has as main objective to permit the therapists the access to the saved information regarding the registered times from the games of reaction and memory in a simple and intuitive way. In this, the information saved in the SD Card is sent to a database and analyzed for all the statistics presented.

In Fig. 4, there is the general and graphical information where it is possible to see the evolution of the player through time. Beside that it is also possible to change all the settings of the game, such as the number of plays for all the games, the buttons in game, the sounds and the volume.

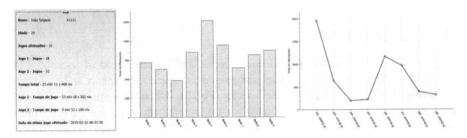

Fig. 4. Different view of information - on the left there is the user information, in the middle there is general graphical information and on the right there is the graphical user profile.

3 Preliminary Tests and Results

The tests were performed in an association with children with special needs, mainly with cerebral palsy and autism. Most of them have similar competences underdeveloped, like the lack of attention, autonomy, cognitive skills and communication. There were three different sessions with each of the ten children supervised by the therapist up to 12 years old (6 boys and 4 girls). They have played the reaction and memory games in all sessions, being the multiplayer game optional. Both games were played using the animals' sounds where the therapists encouraged them to tell the name of the animal before pressing the right button. The sessions took between some seconds and some few minutes depending on the children performance with the presence of the children, the therapist and the researcher.

The feedback of therapists was positive, indicating that this game platform can be useful in the area of occupational therapy. Almost all children have shown moments of concentration in the game and also they enjoyed the playtime. It was possible to note some improvements on the autonomous play, after they understand that pressing the white button they could repeat the selected game.

As an example, Fig. 5 shows the evolution of a child in two different sessions. It is possible to see that in both sessions, along the playtime the player decreases the average time to press the correct button, performing better and keeping focused and entertained.

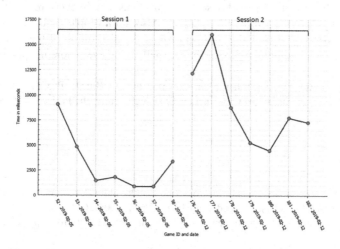

Fig. 5. Evolution graphic from the reaction game in two different sessions: average time to press the correct button.

4 Conclusions and Future Work

The main goal of this on-going work was to develop the first prototype of a configurable toy for children with special needs. Reaction and memory skills as well cooperative work were the designed activities, previously defined in collaboration with the therapists. It is worth pointing out that the therapists are crucial to the game challenges configuration and interface as well as for the game evolution requisites.

The toy is capable of producing audio and visual sensations. The game can be adapted to any child by changing the settings values and all plays are tracked and saved for further analyzed on the application.

The results obtained in the preliminary tests allowed to conclude that the prototype developed may be an interesting tool to work with impaired children in intervention sessions. Also, the audiovisual sensations created are sufficient to keep the children entertained and focused while playing.

Next steps in the research includes, game optimization and well-defined test sessions. In particular, the game improvements include the application of artificial intelligence algorithms in order to automatically adapt the game to each child preferences and performances and continuously motivating for them. It is also important to improve the communication between the game and the interface. A possible solution to this, is to include a wireless communication in real time, and have the application stored in an online server, providing more efficiently the tools needed for the therapists.

Considering the reaction and memory games, the buttons instead of being activated randomly, this could be done by an algorithm that checks the user profile and gets the ones that the player shows low performance.

An optimized solution of the toy would be achieved by substituting each top part of every button by a round LED display that could fit on it and the therapist could choose any image for any button. This would bring more possibilities for the games. As an example, a spell game, where the therapist chooses a list of words, and in every round, the players should click by the correct order the syllables. Also, for a simple game like the reaction game, the possibility of changing in every round the disposition of the images shown could bring another complexity to the game, challenging even more the players.

Acknowledgements. This work has been supported by COMPETE: POCI-01-0145-FEDER-007043 and FCT – Fundação para a Ciência e Tecnologia within the Project Scope: UID/CEC/00319/2019.

References

1. Care, P.: The importance of play in promoting healthy child development and maintaining strong parent-child (2007). https://doi.org/10.1542/peds.2006-2697
2. Help, M.T.: Listen and feel multi-sensory toys help the mind grow strong, pp. 22–26, October 2011
3. Queiroz, N.L.N.D., Maciel, D.A., Branco, A.U.: Brincadeira e desenvolvimento infantil: um olhar sociocultural construtivista. Paidéia (Ribeirão Preto) **16**(34), 169–179 (2006). ISSN: 0103-863X. (in Portuguese)
4. Figueiredo, B.A., De Souza, S., Cristina, A.: Occupational therapy contribution, pp. 29–35 (2016)
5. Hourcade, J.P.: Interaction design and children. Found. Trends® Hum. Comput. Interact. **1**(4), 277–392 (2008)
6. Frauenberger, C., Good, J., Keay-Bright, W.: Designing technology for children with special needs: bridging perspectives through participatory design. CoDesign **7**(1), 1–28 (2011)

7. Hourcade, J.P., Bullock-Rest, N.E., Hansen, T.E.: Multitouch tablet applications and activities to enhance the social skills of children with autism spectrum disorders. Pers. Ubiquit. Comput. **16**(2), 157–168 (2012)
8. Saraiji, M.H.D., et al.: MetaArmS: body remapping using feet-controlled artificial arms. In: The 31st Annual ACM Symposium on User Interface Software and Technology, pp. 65–74. ACM (2018)
9. Atmel, T., Performance, H., Power, L., Avr, A., Family, M.: ATmega328/P (2016)

Digitally-Mediated Learning Environments and Information Literacy for Active Ageing: A Pilot Study

Liliana Vale Costa[1]([✉]), Ana Isabel Veloso[1], and Fernanda Martins[2]

[1] DigiMedia Research Centre, Department of Communication and Art,
University of Aveiro, Campus Universitário de Santigo,
3810-193 Aveiro, Portugal
{lilianavale, aiv}@ua.pt
[2] University of Porto, Via Panorâmica s/n, 4150-564 Porto, Portugal
mmartins@letras.up.pt

Abstract. Over the past few years, the use of Information and Communication Technologies (ICT) in older adults has been an increasing topic of interest within the fields of gerontology and new media. Given the global ageing population, the educational sector has also been challenged in order to meet the learning needs in older adults, age-related changes in cognition and learning, and different learning styles in formal, non-formal or informal contexts. Using the Delphi method with experts to validate the instruments used for data collection, 33 participant surveying and field notes, this study aims to identify the main requirements for designing digitally-mediated learning environments for active ageing. This paper gives an important insight into Educational Gerontology and ICT by understanding the context of the older adult learner and suggesting the following recommendations to enable them to be active constructors of knowledge: (a) combine information delivered in digital devices with face-to-face learning events; (b) intertwine daily-life phenomena with the learning content; (c) offer the possibility to share the learning content with friends and contribute with own content.

Keywords: Digitally-mediated learning environments · Active ageing · Pilot study · Information literacy · Digital inclusion · Learning styles

1 Introduction

In an era of demographic ageing and prevalence of such neurodegenerative diseases as Alzheimer, Parkinson and cerebrovascular diseases [1], there has been an increasingly concern with the genetic and environmental factors that are associated to ageing process, anti-ageing drugs, rehabilitation and the use of digitally-mediated learning interventions to foster active ageing [2, 3]. In fact, the ageing process has aroused the curiosity of Humankind over the years with the attempts made by a number of philosophers to define happiness (e.g. Aristotle), the proposed theories of wellbeing (e.g. Hedonism – Plato in Protagoras) or the concerns with longevity, domestic medicine in the 18th and 19th century [4]. In recent years, a sedentary lifestyle [5], the loss

C. Sylla and I. Iurgel (Eds.): TIE 2019, LNICST 307, pp. 80–90, 2020.
https://doi.org/10.1007/978-3-030-40180-1_9

of muscle mass [6] and the frequency of psychiatric disorders in older adults [7] have led to the need of investigating the use of digitally-mediated interventions to prevent, rehabilitate and contribute to active ageing in the dimensions of health (i.e. physical activity, nutrition, cognition and social activity), sense of security and participation in society [8].

Alongside this concern with active ageing, there has been an interest associated to adult learning for health [9] and the use of Information and Communication Technologies (ICT) in older adult learning and behavior change [10]. Furthermore, it is believed that adult learning has its roots in the 70 s with the author Malcom Knowles [11] (p.2), who defines the field of Andragogy [greek root – andr (man), agogos (learning) and logy (study)] as: "Core principles of adult learning that in turn enables those designing and conducting adult learning to build more effective learning processes for adults." These principles are [11]: the learner's need to know; self-concept of the learner; prior experiences of the learner; readiness to learn; orientation to learning; and motivation.

Relative to the process of learning in later adulthood, the terms of geragogy, gerontagogy [12, 13] or educational gerontology [12, 14] are used in order to characterize the interdependence of such different knowledge bases as: gerontology (geront- old man + logy- study of) and pedagogy (paidios – child + ago – lead + logy – study of) [13] that can occur in formal, non-formal or informal contexts [15]. Whereas formal learning is characterized by hierarchy (i.e. Universities of Third Age, Institutes for learning in retirement or Elderhostels), non-formal and informal learning refers to learning through social groups or networks (e.g. voluntary organizations, churches, sports and clubs) or/and its embeddedness in daily life (e.g. television, games, radio or family background).

It is worth noting that the older adults' access to learning is a right that is recognized in the Second World Assembly on Ageing [16] and initiatives as the Universities of Third Age seem to have a crucial role in the individual's wellbeing and quality of life through communal activities, self-actualization and its interrelationships with the society [17]. In this sense, adopting digital platforms in these contexts may have the potential to extend these formal learning spaces to the daily base, create collaborative and safe learning environments that take into account the learners' pace and confidentiality and may forge intergenerational relationships [17]. The aim of this study is, therefore, to identify the main requirements for designing digitally-mediated learning environments for active ageing.

2   Method

A Participatory Action Research (PAR) was used in order to involve the end-users in the assessment of the requirements for designing digitally-mediated learning environments for active ageing. In specific, this study used the Delphi method with experts to validate the instruments used for data collection, participant surveying and field notes to understand the requirements that would be necessary for designing such a program.

The field work and a set of group discussions to evaluate the learning programs were carried out at the Portuguese Universities of Third Age Gafanha da Nazaré. From March 2015 to December 2016 (2 hr session per week), the researcher lectured about ICT and Active ageing in order to gain the participants' confidence, commitment and trust and assess both the learning context and motivations to learn.

2.1 Participants

Thirty-three out of thirty-seven participants were involved in this survey, regarding the fact that four did not meet the selection criteria (1 did not fit within the age bracket and 3 did not complete all sessions). The criteria used for selecting the participants in this study were: (a) being aged 50 and over; (b) know how to read and write; (c) voluntary participation; and (d) interest in learning. The sample was gender-balanced (51.5% female and 48.5% male), the average age was 67 years old (SD = 7.06; minimum = 55; maximum = 82) and the majority of the participants had between 10 and 14 years of schooling. Forty adult learners at four Universities of Third Age then tested two digitally-mediated learning programs (a game-based learning – GBLP and a computer-assisted learning program – CALP) for active ageing in order to define the requirements for designing digitally-mediated learning environments for active ageing. Twenty participants (50% female and 50% male, M = 73 years old, SD = 5.93) tested firstly the GBLP and then the CALP whereas other 20 (60% female and 40% male, M = 69 years old, SD = 7.16) tested firstly the CALP and then the GBLP, aiming at not creating some bias relative to the order in which the learning programs were presented.

The study has been approved by the Ethics Committee of the University of Aveiro (Resolution n.3/2015) that safeguards, among other things: the informed consent of the participants aged 50 and over; voluntary participation; involvement of the research team in the process; and that the risks do not outweigh the risks associated with the participants' daily lives.

2.2 Measures and Procedures

Before assessing the participants' perceived learning motivation and styles, the surveys and content provided relative to the domains of active ageing [8]- i.e. health, security and participation in society were reviewed in terms of the quality of the materials and the procedures to be undertaken in the fieldwork by a group of experts in the fields of Gerontology, Psychology, Education and Social Work. These planned sessions embodied the following themes:

1. Presentation of the Research Project;
2. Physical Activity;
3. Nutrition;
4. Cognitive Activity;
5. Sense of Security; and
6. Participation in Society.

These sessions would enable to have access to the participants' context in order to design a digitally-mediated learning program for active ageing. In terms of the planned sessions, the criteria used were the following:

- The goals presented were/were not specific, measurable, achievable and time-based;
- The content covered/did not cover essential topics related with the concept of Active Ageing;
- The module was/was not sufficient and clear;
- There was/was not a risk of multiple interpretations or ambiguity in the use of terms;
- The sequence in which the content presented was/was not the most appropriate;
- There were/were not terms that needed explanation;
- The subject was/was not in-depth, in view of the objectives presented;
- The language used was/was not clear and accessible;
- The content was/was not updated;
- The literature presented was/was not relevant to support the arguments presented.

Relative to the survey, the criteria were the following:

- The scope and the purpose of the research were/were not explained;
- The instructions were/were not sufficiently and clearly described;
- There was/was not risk of multiple interpretations or ambiguity in the use of terms;
- The sequence of the questions;
- Suitability of the questions to each section;
- Number of repeated or inappropriate questions;
- Terms that needed explanation;
- Adequacy of the scale used;
- Suitability of the questions formulated for the analysis; and
- Validity of the content in scientific terms.

The objective of the survey was to assess the participants' context relative to the learning process in order to find the best strategy to transmit the information about active ageing in both digitally-mediated platforms.

After validating these instruments for data collection, the learning sessions at a University of Third Age were carried out *in loco*, aiming at understanding the current participants' learning context. In the specific case of learning motivations, preferences and styles, a questionnaire was self-administered that covered the following topics: The motivation to adhere to a learning program ('What motivates you to adhere to a learning program?'), in which the participants were given a list of possible reasons why they might adhere to the program ('Pleasure and fun', 'Relax', 'Pass time', 'Meet new people and make friendships', 'Increment participation in activities', 'Update skills at work', 'Foster life-long learning', 'Encourage intergenerational learning', 'Personal fulfilment', and 'Prevent or lessen the severity of certain diseases – e.g. Alzheimer, dementia'), including the 'Other';

The participants' learning style was assessed based on a set of sentences that were categorized into the theories: Behaviorism (BH), Cognitivism (CG) and Constructivism

(CT). The statements relative to Behaviorism (BH) were: 1. 'My surroundings affect my learning process (e.g. place, people...)'; 2. 'New apprenticeships influence my behaviors', 3. 'I like that the goals of the training activities, which I participate, are presented.', 4. 'I learn a lot through observation of others' behaviors, attitudes and herein consequences'.

In Cognitivism (CG), the following items were used: 'I like when schemas are presented relative to the learning content', 'I learn better if words and images are displayed rather than only images', 'Learning is a discovery process', 'Emotions have a strong influence on my learning process', 'My success in training activities depends on my effort', 'My success in training activities depends on the difficulty level of the task', 'My success in training depends on the luck factor', 'I often select only the information that interests me', 'I like to start with simple challenges and then move to the difficult ones' and 'I like examples to be presented about what I am learning.'

Finally, the following statements were formulated based on the Constructivism theory (CT): 'I like to participate in group activities', 'I like to build my own knowledge', 'I enjoy sharing information with people who have common interests', 'I enjoy learning challenges', 'I enjoy learning challenges that meet my learning capacities'. Associated to constructivism (CT), the social component is also important and, therefore, the following statements were added: 'I like to use Information and Communication Technologies (ICT) to learn and share information' and 'I enjoy sharing knowledge with the same interests as me.' The list of reasons that could lead the participants to adhere to a learning program were based on the Political declaration and Madrid International Plan of Action on Ageing [18], the Hamburg Declaration on Adult Learning [19] and the Andragogical principles proposed by Knowles, Holton and Swanson [11], in which the following recommendations were related with the proposed statements:

(a) Create collaborative and safe environments – 'Meet new people and make new friends' and 'Increment participation in activities';
(b) Adapt adult learning to changing world of work – 'Update skills at work', 'Foster life-long learning';
(c) Meet the learners' self-concept and take into account the learners' pace and confidentiality – 'Improve self- esteem', 'Pleasure and fun', 'Relax', 'Pass time', 'Personal fulfilment'
(d) Foster self-direct learning and take into account the ageing factors – 'Prevent or lessen the severity of certain diseases'; and
(e) Motivate adult learners to produce their own learning artefacts and share them with younger generations – 'Encourage intergenerational learning'.

Relative to the learning styles, these were based on different theories:

• Behaviorism: Relative to this theory, the willing that learners' behaviors can be shaped by different stimulus and positive or negative reinforcements was illustrated in the statement 'My surroundings affect my learning process – e.g. place, people...'; the interrelationship between learning and behaviors was covered in 'New apprenticeships influence my behaviors' whereas the design of goal-oriented learning program (GOMS – Goals, Operators, Methods, Selection, Rules model) was relative to 'I like that the goals of the training activities, which I participate, are presented' and the process of observational learning was covered in 'I learn a lot through observation of others' behaviors, attitudes and herein consequences.'

- Cognitivism: The learner is seen as an information processor and learning is based on mental constructions of daily life events and symbols, being words and pictures also important in comparison with words – 'I like when schemas are presented relative to the learning content', 'I learn better if words and images are displayed rather than only images' and 'Learning is a discovery process.' The influence of emotions in the learning process are illustrated in the following sentences: 'Emotions have a strong influence on my learning process', 'My success in training activities depends on my effort', 'My success in training activities depends on the difficulty level of the task' and 'My success in training depends on the luck factor.' The Cognitive Theory of Multimedia Learning, in which the learning process is dependent on the process of filtering, selecting, organizing and manipulating information is covered in the following statements: 'I often select only the information that interests me' and 'I like to start with simple challenges and then move to the difficult ones.' The situated cognition principle that refers to the interconnection between the learning content and the individuals' daily life is then alluded to the statement 'I like examples to be presented about what I am learning.'
- Constructivism: In constructivism, learners are seen as active constructors of their own knowledge and the learning process is challenge or problem driven. This process of self-discovery were then reflected in the following statements: 'I like to participate in group activities', 'I like to build my own knowledge', 'I enjoy sharing information with people who have common interests', 'I enjoy learning challenges that meet my learning capacities.'

Finally, social interactions and Communities of practices are both related with the process of constructing knowledge and connectivism and as such, the following statements were added: 'I like to use Information and Communication Technologies (ICT) to learn and share information' and 'I enjoy sharing knowledge with people with the same interests as me.' For each statement, the participants had to rate them, using the scale from 1 (1 = totally disagree) to 5 (5 = totally agree). Two digitally-mediated learning programs that covered the dimensions of Active ageing – Health (Physical activity, Cognitive activity, Nutrition), Security and Participation in Society were then developed and the participants' perceived strengths, weaknesses and suggestions for improvement in both the learning platforms were registered using field notes.

The learning process is then centered on missions that can be both accomplished both in-game and in the physical space. Depending on the player's activity, he/she can be rewarded by each mission through the use of experience points (ranking), being able to discuss the learning content with other players through an off-game discussing area. These different functionalities meet the principles that were proposed by Gee [9]: empowering learners (through identity, offering a personal discovery through missions and enabling learners to interact with a digital environment; problem-solving by enabling scaffolding in missions and monitoring them through rewards, presenting information 'just in time' and associating the gameplay activity to skills and experience points; and deep understanding by intertwining the information provided to the learners' context and activity as well as a certain point of time and place. Figure 1 shows an example of a mission related with Nutrition, in which the adult learners have to guess in which card the food with a certain vitamin is hidden.

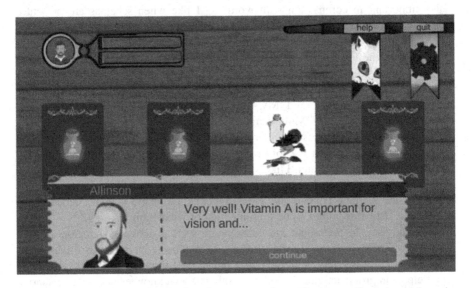

Fig. 1. Minigame related with the learning content about Nutrition - Game-based Learning Programme (GBLP)

In relation to the Computer-assisted Learning Program (CALP), the learning process in the is divided into the following areas: Learning, Rewards/Analytics, Learning Plan and Social. In specific, the CALP stores information relative to the learner (name. date, email, password, photo and description) and (s)he can create multiple events and posts that are dependent on the learning course. A task-based system is then associated to trophies and on-demand doubts that are posed the adult learners. This system operates the following recommendations: (a) an audio-visual strategy that gets the learner familiar with the source of information – learning profile, mentoring and on-demand doubts; (b) foster self-knowledge with the learning profile and the possibility of creating events (learning plan); (c) reward task-management through the interrelationship between the individual activities and the area of badges and trophies; and (d) build a community of practice through the area of sharing, in which learners can share their views on the learning content and share doubts relative to a certain minute of the video. Figure 2 shows an example of a video of the online course.

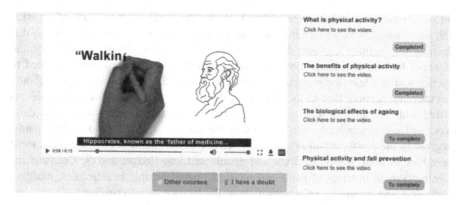

Fig. 2. Video of the online course

The learning content is delivered through an audiovisual strategy, in which the participants can send their doubts to the instructor depending on the time they are at the moment by clicking 'I have a doubt'. Both learning programs are available on the following links: Game-based learning - jump.web.ua.pt and Computer-assisted learning – seriousgiggle.web.ua.pt (Access date: January 16th, 2019).

An observation protocol was then used for each session, being structured as follows: reference number, place, date and time, activity and goals, portraits/description of the main actions with the participants' statements and references to audio-visual materials/photos/documents.

3   Results

When surveying the participants about their main motivations to adhere to a digitally mediated learning program, these were: foster life-long learning (N = 28, 84.8%); and improve self-esteem, self-confidence, cognitive capacity and personal fulfilment (N = 21, 93.9%). Furthermore, only four out of the thirty-three adult learners, who were interviewed (12.1%), have enrolled a course delivered at distance and the main reasons that they have pointed out were: flexibility in schedules; and personalization of the learning programs to the learner's context. In relation to the perception towards the different learning styles, Table 1 shows its popularity towards the participants. As can be shown in Table 1, the adult learners are likely to prefer learning environments that would enable them to be active constructors of their own knowledge challenge or problem driven. Learning environments addressed to the adults aged 50 and over should, therefore, enable self-discovery (M = 4.43, SD = 0.68), display words and images rather than only images (M = 4.43; SD = 0.63) and present schemas relative to the learning content (M = 4.26, SD = 0.82). In fact, constructivism tends to be the learning style that mostly suits the participants (the mean was 4 points or over to 6 out 8 sentences).

When observing the participants and discussing about the main strengths and weaknesses of both learning platforms relative to the different functionalities, the following recommendations were added: 1. Enable the participants to share information with those who have common interests and present multimodal texts and schemas that illustrate the learning content: 2. Prioritize problem-solving (strategy), memory and attention, logic and reaction time as cognitive skills that the participants wanted to practice with the learning program; 3. The digitally-mediated learning program should also take into account face-to-face learning events –e.g. round tables, solving problems related with the learning content and get challenges that are intertwined with daily lives, and contribute with own content to the course; 4. Monitor the participants' progress in the platform and reward their activity in the platform in order bring some incentives to their learning efforts and enable self-knowledge; and 5. Organise the learning content in terms of goals and missions, being flexible in schedules, enabling scaffolding and providing information about the 'source of information.'

Table 1. Participants' perception towards their learning style (L.Style)

L.Style	Sentences	Mean	SD
BH	1. My surroundings affect my learning process (e.g. place, people...)	3.77	1.14
	2. New apprenticeships influence my behaviours	3.07	1.19
	3. I like that the goals of training activities, which I participate, are presented	4.21	0.77
	4. I learn a lot through observation of others' behaviours, attitudes and herein consequences	4.10	0.72
CG	5. I like when schemas are presented relative to the learning content	4.26	0.82
	6. I learn better if words and images are displayed rather than only images	4.43	0.63
	7. Learning is a discovery process	4.43	0.68
	8. Emotions have a strong influence on my learning process	3.87	1.01
	9. My success in training activities depends on my effort	4.10	0.99
	10. My success in training activities depends on the difficulty level of the task	3.68	1.08
	11. My success in training activities depends on the luck factor	2.23	1.22
	12. I often select only the information that interests me	3.59	1.27
	13. I like to start with simple challenges and then move on to the more difficult ones	3.97	0.91
	14. I like examples to be presented about what I am learning	4.19	0.93
CT	15. I like to participate in group activities	4.06	0.99
	16. I like to build my own knowledge	3.88	0.98
	16. I enjoy sharing information with people who have common interests	4.31	0.93
	17. I enjoy learning challenges	4.00	0.95
	18. I like to solve problems based on previous experiences	4.19	0.89
	19. I like to use Information and Communication Technologies (ICT) to learn and share information	3.81	1.01
	20. I enjoy sharing knowledge with people with the same interests as me	4.25	0.92
	21. I enjoy learning challenges that meet my learning capacities	4.03	0.95

4   Discussion

This study set out to identify the main requirements for designing digitally-mediated learning environments for active ageing, in which the ultimate goal is the individual's well-being and quality of life. Based on the use of the Delphi method with experts to validate the instruments used for data collection, 33 participant surveying and field notes, the following requirements are suggested: (a) combine information delivered in digital devices with face-to-face learning events; (b) intertwine daily-life phenomena with the learning content; and (c) offer the possibility to share the learning content with friends and contribute with own content. Furthermore, the adult learners are likely to prefer learning environments that would enable them to be active constructors of their own knowledge challenge or problem driven and as such, these programmes should enable self-discovery and present schemas relative to the learning content. In fact, adopting digital platforms in these contexts may have the potential to extend these formal learning spaces to the daily base, create collaborative and safe learning environments that take into account the learners' pace and confidentiality and may forge intergenerational relationships. Future work is being carried out in order to explore the adaption of these requirements to the context of an online community.

Acknowledgements. We want to thank all the participants and Universities of Third Age that collaborated with us in this project. This work was supported by FCT (Fundação para a Ciência e Tecnologia), COMPETE 2020, Portugal 2020 and EU through the European Regional Development Fund – the project SEDUCE 2.0 nr. POCI-01-0145-FEDER-031696.

References

1. Hindle, J.V.: Ageing, neurodegeneration and Parkinson's disease. Age Ageing **39**(2), 156–161 (2010). https://doi.org/10.1093/ageing/afp223
2. Bouma, H., Fozard, J.L., Taipale, V.: Gerontotechnology in perspective. Gerontotechnology **6**(4), 190–216 (2007)
3. Costa, L.: Game-based learning for Active Ageing. Doctoral thesis, University of Aveiro, Aveiro, Portugal (2017)
4. Cheyne, G.: An Essay of Health and Long Life. Arno Press, New York (1724)
5. Burton, L.C., et al.: The effect among older persons of a general preventive visit on three health behaviors: smoking, excessive alcohol drinking, and sedentary lifestyle. Prev. Med. **24**(5), 492–497 (1995). https://doi.org/10.1006/pmed.1995.1078
6. Grönstedt, H., et al.: A study protocol of Older Person's Exercise and Nutrition Study (OPEN) - a sit-to-stand activity combined with oral protein supplement – effects on physical function and independence: a cluster randomized clinical trial. BMC Geriatr. **18**(138), 1–10 (2018). https://doi.org/10.1186/s12877-018-0824-1
7. Seitz, D., Purandare, N., Conn, D.: Prevalence of psychiatric disorders among older adults in long-term care homes: a systematic review. Int. Psychogeriatr. **22**(7), 1025–1039 (2010). https://doi.org/10.1017/S1041610210000608
8. WHO - World Health Organization.: Active ageing: A policy framework, pp. 5–55. World Health Organization, Geneva (2002)

9. Feinstein, L., Hammond, C.: The contribution of adult learning to health and social capital. Oxf. Rev. Educ. **30**(2), 199–221 (2004)
10. Glanz, K., Rimer, B., Viswanath, K.: Health Behavior and Health: Theory, Research and Practice. Wiley, San Francisco (2008)
11. Knowles, M.S., Holton, E.F., Swanson, R.A.: The Adult Learner. Routledge, New York (2012)
12. Findsen, B., Formosa, M.: Rationales for older adult learning, In: Lifefong Learning in Later Life, pp. 89–101. SensePublishers (2011). https://doi.org/10.1007/978-94-6091-651-9_8
13. Lemieux, A., Martinez, M.: Gerontagogy beyond word: a reality. Educ. Gerontol. **26**(5), 475–498 (2000)
14. Peterson, D.A.: Educational gerontology: the state of the art. Educ. Gerontol. **1**(1), 61–68 (1976)
15. Jarvis, P.: Sociological perspective on lifelong education and lifelong learning, Department of Adult Education, University of Georgia, Athens (1985)
16. UN - United Nations: Universal Declaration of Human Rights (1948). http://www.un.org/en/universal-declaration-human-rights/. Accessed 12 June 2019
17. Czaja, S.J., Sharit, J.: Designing Training and Instructional Programs for Older Adults. CRC, Boca Raton (2012)
18. UN-United Nations: Political Declaration and Madrid International Plan of Action on Ageing, Madrid (2002)
19. UNESCO, Adult Education – The Hamburg declaration the agenda for the future, UNESCO (1997)

European Video Game Development and Disability: Reflections on Data, Rights, Decisions and Assistance

Benedikt Pielenz[✉]

Technische Universität Darmstadt, Alexanderstr. 6, 64289 Darmstadt, Germany
benedikt.pielenz@gmail.com

Abstract. The *European Union* (EU) is funding the development of computer games for people with disabilities since 2004. Since 2014, the *Education, Audiovisual and Culture Executive Age*ncy (EACEA) – as part of the EU – is responsible for the management of development and funding of European Video Games. In 2010 the European Disability Strategy has taken effect. Ever since, the integration of people with disabilities into cultural life as well as learning environments has become one of the main topics in the EU. As computer games are part of both – cultural life and learning environments – the link between people with disabilities and video games are being reflected and discussed in this paper. The results show, that on the one hand the responsibility of the EU and EACEA to include people with disabilities into the development of computer games is taken into account. On the other hand, there is a lack of current quantitative data on people with disabilities playing video games and it remains difficult to say how many people face exclusion. Moreover, assistive technologies are still a niche product. Due to their expensiveness as well as their non-plug-and-play usability, they frequently remain difficult to use. Nevertheless, possibilities to link inclusion and technology in educational environments do exist.

Keywords: Disability game studies · European video game industry · European video game development · People with disabilities · Assistive technologies · Inclusive programming

1 Introduction

Over forty-five years ago, PONG (1972) became the world's first popular digital game[1] [10]. The popularity of video games is ongoing in public and academic discussions, ever since. Social projects like the newspaper strassen gazette refer to them under their aspects of social inclusion[2]. But academics are interested in the inclusional facets of computer games, too. The list of publications about the positive influences of video games, for example on people with disabilities, is current and diverse [7, 18].

---

[1] Hereinafter also referred to as video games and computer games.

[2] German newspaper sold by people without a permanent home. Issue of September 2019.

© ICST Institute for Computer Sciences, Social Informatics and Telecommunications Engineering 2020
Published by Springer Nature Switzerland AG 2020. All Rights Reserved
C. Sylla and I. Iurgel (Eds.): TIE 2019, LNICST 307, pp. 91–97, 2020.
https://doi.org/10.1007/978-3-030-40180-1_10

Nevertheless, the reactions on computer games vary from hype to skepticism [14]. One reason for the divergency in opinions is probably the popularity of video games.

In Germany, the Southwest Media Education Research Network is collecting data on a regular basis. Data about the participation of children (6–13 yrs.) in digital games is being collected since 1999 (n = 537) and youngsters (12–19 yrs.) since 1998 (n = 568) [11, 12]. The past twenty years show, that the participation in video games has risen ever since.

In Austria, a first and last bigger data collection (n = 3.002) took place in 2017. It was commissioned by the Austrian Association for Entertainment Software[3]. The headline states, that almost two thirds of the 7.3 million online-households do play video games. To sum up, Germany and Austria are both interested in collecting data on participation in digital games. However, they share a lack of interest in data collection on people with disabilities playing computer games. An online-survey from 2008 (n = 13.296) shows, over twenty percent of people playing video games identify themselves as disabled[4]. Even if a general interest in the people playing video games exists, there is no special interest in people with disabilities playing computer games [1]. All in all, there is room for research, discussion and reflection left. To guide this first conclusion, the upcoming article takes a look onto the following questions: Why is it necessary to dis- cuss the link between people with disabilities and computer games? How are digital games and disabilities being faced together in the development of European Video Games? Where are possibilities and difficulties for technical inclusion?

2 The Human Right to Play in Austria and Germany

Members of the *European Union* (EU) must follow the *Universal Declaration of Human Rights* (UDHR). An agreement, that regulates these rights especially for people with disabilities is the *Convention on the Rights of Persons with Disabilities* (CRPD). For this paper, the Article 30 is especially interesting. It states, that children must be enabled to participate in culture and play without barriers [15]. For Austria, the CRPD came into effect on the 26th October 2008 and for Germany on the 26th March 2009. The EU addressed the rights of persons with disabilities with the *European Strategy for People with Disabilities* (ESPD) in 2010 and 2014[5].

As mentioned in the CRPD and ESPD, there is a right to cultural participation for people with disabilities. As computer games are part of European culture[6], there is a right for barrier free participation. As people with disabilities have a right to participate

---

[3] https://www.ovus.at/news/fast-5-millionen-osterreicher-spielen-videogames/.

[4] https://www.gamesindustry.biz/articles/popcap-games-research-publisher-s-latest-survey-says-that-casual-games-are-big-with-disabled-people/.

[5] Reference: European Disability Strategy 2010–2020.

[6] Reference: L 347/221.

in video games, there is a need to address these rights. Therefore, the next chapter focuses on the development of European Video Games supported by the *Education, Audiovisual and Culture Executive Agency* (EACEA).

3 Supporting the Development of European Video Games

In this chapter, the support of the EU and EACEA regarding people with disabilities playing video games is being focussed. One of the main aspects of computer games is them being played. As a result, people playing them are a key aspect in their development [13]. As mentioned in the chapter before, people with disability have a right to participate in video games. But even before the ESPD started in 2010, the EU funded projects focussing people with disabilities and video games. One of the first could be backdated to 2004. Even if the project *Guidelines for the development of entertaining software for people with multiple learning disabilities* (UPS) was cancelled right after the official beginning[7], the research on *Methods for Prototype Testing of Inclusive Computer Games* in the same year was not [19]. Eight years later (2012), the non-profit- project *Game Accessibility Guidelines*[8] began to support the video game industry with tips and tricks about the inclusion of people with disabilities into video games. In addition, even *Microsoft* published tips and tricks for barrier free games in 2017[9].

In between the EACEA started the funding of European Video Games and their funding with 2.5 million euro each year (max. 250.000 Euro per project). The program started in 2013 and will end in 2020[10]. Guidelines on how to get funded are being published online since 2014 and people with disabilities are being focussed as well since 2015[11]. Regarding to the guidelines, the developed games should suit the target audience. For example, the developers get five points for the inclusion of accessibility features which enhance the accessibility for gamers with disabilities. Altogether, there are one-hundred points to get.

As the EU decided to include computer games into their cultural heritage, nearly 1000 (n = 996) games were submitted to the EACEA for their support from 2014 to 2019 (see footnote 6). Furthermore, developers from 33 European countries[12] participated in the application process in the same period. More detailed information about nine out of the 33 countries participated in recent years could be found in Table 1.

---

[7] http://www.medialt.no/rapport/entertainment_guidelines/.

[8] http://gameaccessibilityguidelines.com/.

[9] https://docs.microsoft.com/en-us/windows/uwp/gaming/accessibility-for-games.

[10] Reference: C (2013) 8314 of 28 November 2013.

[11] References: EAC/S31/2013, EACEA/06/2015, EACEA/20/2015, EACEA/22/2016, EACEA/24/2017 and EACEA/24/2018.

[12] Austria, Belgium, Bosnia and Herzegovina, Bulgaria, Croatia, Cyprus, Czech Republic, Den- mark, Estonia, Germany, Greece, Finland, France, Hungary, Iceland, Ireland, Italy, Latvia, Lithuania, Malta, Netherlands, Norway, Poland, Portugal, Republic of Macedonia, Romania, Serbia, Slovakia, Slovenia, Spain, Sweden, Switzerland and United Kingdom.

Even if successful submissions do not exceed 23% in any year and the applications received have almost halved, the success rate has doubled from the beginning on.

In short, tips, tricks and guidelines for the inclusion of people with disabilities into computer game development do exist. They are provided by non-profit-organisations as well as the software industry. Besides, the EU has a special interest in funding projects regarding people with disabilities and video game development. European departments like the EACEA try to channel the growth and capabilities of computer games since 2013. But they could focus on inclusion even more. For example, there is no real need for developers of European Video Games to include accessibility futures into the final video game. Instead, they could focus another European audience at will not lose any points. Nevertheless, possibilities to participate even in finished games do exist. For instance, assistive technologies help people with disabilities to participate in video games, as shown in the next chapter.

4 Assistive Technology as a Chance for Inclusion

Computer games are designed for play and so are assistive technologies, as one of the common subtasks using assistive technologies is participating in computer games [9]. Video game worlds are an educational tool and technology can make a difference for students with disabilities to participate in these learning environments [5, 6]. The importance of barrier free participation through assistive technology was taken into account by the EU in 2010 and 2019[13]. Nonetheless, the devices may need to be rebuilt from scratch, as plug-and-play technologies are rare [8].

According to a report about the European assistive technology industry, they often do require readjustments as well as maintenance before, during and after their installation [17]. Nevertheless, there are fine working assistive technologies for playing computer games in existence [4, 16]. For example, the blind use haptic displays and talking dictionaries since at least 2003 [2, 9]. Even electric-wheelchair-joysticks, that are familiar to gaming-joysticks, are commonly used [3]. Besides, guidelines – not only for computer game development as mentioned in chapter three – for the use and development of assistive technologies do exist [6].

In conclusion, assistive technologies are being used by people with disabilities to play computer games and are an important tool for inclusion in learning environments. The EU is interested in assistive technologies as shown in critical evaluations and recent strategies. In addition, there is a general interest in technical inclusion of people with disabilities. Regarding the findings on participation, human rights, computer game development and assistive technology, the next chapter will conclude and discuss those topics.

---

[13] Reference: PE/81/2018/REV/1.

Table 1. Applications by country (selection of 33 countries participated in total)

	2014		2015		2016		2017		2018		2019	
	AR[a]	ASR[a]	AR	ASR	AR	ASR	AR	ASR	AR	ASR	AR	ASR
Austria	5	20%	2	0%	3	0%	3	33%	0	0%	2	0%
Belgium	5	0%	2	50%	1	0%	0	0%	3	33%	2	50%
Czech Republic	6	17%	0	0%	6	17%	5	0%	0	0%	1	0%
Germany	25	16%	13	15%	13	31%	15	27%	17	41%	20	40%
Finland	21	10%	6	33%	7	0%	11	0%	9	11%	6	17%
France	24	17%	18	17%	15	7%	12	42%	9	22%	15	20%
Portugal	4	0%	2	0%	1	100%	0	0%	1	0%	3	0%
Slovakia	5	0%	6	0%	5	0%	1	0%	1	0%	2	0%
United Kingdom	27	4%	22	18%	11	9%	24	25%	16	13%	12	17%
Sum	*122*	*9%*	*71*	*15%*	*62*	*18%*	*71*	*14%*	*56*	*13%*	*63*	*16%*
All participants	**259**	**11%**	**182**	**17%**	**138**	**18%**	**146**	**22%**	**132**	**23%**	**139**	**22%**

[a]AR = Applications received, ASR = Average success rate.

5 Discussion

Three questions were asked in the beginning and will be focused in the upcoming discussion. In Germany, there is repeatedly updated quantitative data about kids and teenagers playing video games. In Austria, there is only one bigger collection of data about people playing computer games to be found. What both countries share is a lack of data about people with disabilities playing computer games. There is only one large American survey in existence from 2008 and it is no longer available for further investigation. As participation in video games is a human right, further questions arise. Even if the EU and EACEA do support computer game development regarding people with disabilities in projects since 2004, there is more to do. On the one hand, the submission guidelines of the EACEA do encourage a focus on disability and impairments in the development of European Video Games. On the other hand, there is no real need to implement accessibility features in the computer games and assistive technologies are not mentioned in the guidelines itself. As assistive technologies do make a difference in the inclusion of people with disabilities in video games and therefore learning environments, there is a need for action. Besides, there is a need to strengthen the focus on assistive technologies in upcoming projects for digital game development.

In a more practical fashion, there are possibilities and necessities to integrate and install assistive technologies into more classrooms. Projects or courses aiming on *inclusive programming* tasks could be used in educational environments. Inclusive programming revers to the link between social inclusion and computer science. As mentioned in chapter four, assistive technologies as well as computer games need working hard- and software to function correctly. In addition, they are both being programmed in their development and need to be synchronized. In an inclusive programming project or course, the participants with or without disabilities could improve their programming and social skills by working together. Moreover, they could learn to program their own digital game worlds and assistive technologies for playful and game-based learning as well as reprogram existing video games for more accessibility and usability.

References

1. Bosse, I., Hasebrink, U.: Mediennutzung von Menschen mit Behinderungen (2016). https://www.aktion-mensch.de/dam/jcr:8b186ca0-b0f1-46f8-acb1-a59f295b5bb4/aktion-mensch-studie-mediennutzung-langfassung-2017-03.pdf. 20 August 2019
2. Burdea, G.C., Coiffet, P.: Virtual Reality Technology. Wiley, New York (2003)
3. Carney, J., Dix, C.: Integrating assistive technology in the classroom and community. In: Church, G., Glennen, S. (eds.) The Handbook of Assistive Technology, pp. 207–240. Singular Publishing Group Inc., San Diego (1992)
4. Craddock, G.: Opportunity for change. Assistive technology: a national and European perspective (2005)
5. Girard, C., Ecalle, J., Magnan, A.: Serious games as new educational tools: how effective are they? A meta-analysis of recent studies. J. Comput. Assist. Learn. **29**(3), 207–219 (2013). https://doi.org/10.1111/j.1365-2729.2012.00489.x
6. Green, R.A., Blair, V.: Keep It Simple. A Guide to Assistive Technologies. Libraries Unlimited, Santa Barbara (2011)
7. Griffiths, M.D.: The therapeutic and health benefits of playing video games. In: Atrill-Smith, A., Fullwood, C., Keep, M., Kuss, D.J. (eds.) The Oxford Handbook of Cyberpsychology, pp. 484–505. Oxford University Press, Oxford (2019)
8. Hallewell Haslwanter, J.D., Fitzpatrick, G.: Why do few assistive technology systems make it to market? The case of the HandyHelper project. Univ. Access Inf. Soc. **16**(3), 755–773 (2017). https://doi.org/10.1007/s10209-016-0499-3
9. Hersh, M.A., Johnson, M.A.: Assistive Technology for Visually Impaired and Blind People. Springer, London (2008). https://doi.org/10.1007/978-1-84628-867-8
10. Kirriemuir, J.: A history of digital games. In: Rutter, J., Bryce, J. (eds.) Understanding Digital Games, pp. 21–35. Sage Publications, Thousand Oaks (2006)
11. Medienpädagogischer Forschungsverbund Südwest (1998–2018): JIM-Studie. https://www.mpfs.de/studien/?tab=tab-18-1. 20 August 2019
12. Medienpädagogischer Forschungsverbund Südwest (1999–2018): KIM-Studie. https://www.mpfs.de/studien/?tab=tab-18-2. 20 August 2019
13. Mildner, P., Mueller, F.: Design of serious games. In: Dörner, R., Göbel, S., Effelsberg, W., Wiemeyer, J. (eds.) Serious Games. Foundations, Concepts and Practice, pp. 57–82. Springer, Switzerland (2016). https://doi.org/10.1007/978-3-319-40612-1_3
14. Moore, C.J.: Making moral choices in video games. Christ. Reflect.: A Ser. Faith Ethics **38**, 69–77 (2011)
15. Nikoltchev, S.: Enabling access to the media for all. Strasbourg: European Audiovisual Observatory (Iris plus, 2014-3) (2014). https://rm.coe.int/1680783db1. 20 August 2019
16. Powlik, J.J., Karshmer, A.I.: When accessibility meets usability. Univ. Access Inf. Soc. **1**(3), 217–222 (2002). https://doi.org/10.1007/s10209-002-0020-z
17. Stack, J., et al.: Analysing and federating the European assistive technology ICT industry (2009). https://www.ifap.ru/pr/2009/n090430b.pdf. 20 August 2019

18. Tarakci, D., Ersoz Huseyinsinoglu, B., Tarakci, E., Razak Ozdincler, A.: Effects of Nintendo Wii-Fit® video games on balance in children with mild cerebral palsy. Pediatr. Int. **58**(10), 1042–1050 (2016). https://doi.org/10.1111/ped.12942
19. van Leeuwen, L., Power, A., Ellis, P.: Choosing methods for prototype testing of inclusive computer games. In: Miesenberger, K., Klaus, J., Zagler, W.L., Burger, D. (eds.) ICCHP 2004. LNCS, vol. 3118, pp. 264–271. Springer, Heidelberg (2004). https://doi.org/10.1007/978-3-540-27817-7_40

Innovating Methods

From Big Data Communities to Enterprising Villagers

The Transformational Effect of a Designerly Approach Within a Research Project

Judith van de Goor[✉], Koen van Turnhout, Marjolein Regterschot,
Michel Hansma, and René Bakker

Department of Information Technology, Communication and Media,
HAN University of Applied Sciences, Ruitenberglaan 26,
6826 CC Arnhem, The Netherlands
{Judith.vandeGoor, Koen.vanTurnhout,
Marjolein.Regterschot, Michel.Hansma,
Rene.Bakker}@han.nl

Abstract. Using a designerly approach in projects within a wide spectrum of disciplines is increasingly popular. This paper describes a case in where the 1:10:100 design approach is used in a social sciences project and explores the mutual learning that took place. It discusses the added value of using design artefacts (prototypes) in the process and to what level these can be seen as boundary objects. Among the project partners there are two teams of social scientists (German and Dutch) that were collecting data and worked with abstract thinking processes and a design team who concerned about usability and intervened with design tools. The prototypes in the project are reviewed as boundary objects on three levels: to create common ground, to sharpen focus and as window into the future. The learning mechanisms that occurred (reflection and transformation) shifted the focus in the project from mining data on behalf of a community database towards a tool in which enterprising villagers can show their qualities and entrepreneurship.

Keywords: Designerly approach · Boundary objects · 1:10:100 · Design thinking · Prototypes

1 Introduction

What does a designerly approach bring to an open-ended social sciences project and what role do design artifacts fulfill in this process? Can they function as boundary objects and bridge the cultural differences between the project partners with social sciences and design backgrounds?

This paper explores these questions through a case study around a German-Dutch project called KRAKE DNA. In this project, a team of both German and Dutch social scientists worked together to develop a (digital) tool that maps the DNA of villages in the border region between these two countries. The term DNA refers to the fundamental

C. Sylla and I. Iurgel (Eds.): TIE 2019, LNICST 307, pp. 101–108, 2020.
https://doi.org/10.1007/978-3-030-40180-1_11

factors of success for the sustainability of a village [6], but it is at the start of the project not specified what these fundamental factors of success are or mean. In good cooperation the team of social scientists started the quest how to deal with this assignment. The 'comfortable' way of working for social scientists is to do in-depth research and explore possibilities from within the process. But the project is challenged by different levels of complexity, such as an ill-defined character of the goal, a fuzzy process and a bi-national approach. Witnessing these struggles as a design team, we felt a designerly approach might offer a way forward, although we weren't quite sure how and to what extend this could work.

The KRAKE DNA project offered us the opportunity to explore this approach in a social science research project. The typical project approach for designers is quite different from other disciplines [5]. The social scientists in this project tend to work top-down and are very good at organizing data collection, but new to working with prototypes and creative tools to explore the aspired outcomes of a project. For us as designers it is quite common to work cross-disciplinary, but it was new to look at the 'design artefacts' [1] created in the project as boundary objects that served as a catalyst on a process level. By using a design approach and boundary objects to stimulate conversation and book progress, the project shifted from a focus on datamining to a focus on the entrepreneurial villagers. In this paper we explore the mutual learning that took place and how prototypes as boundary objects supported this transformation.

2   1:10:100 Approach

The goal to develop a (digital) tool to map the DNA of villages in the border region, without having a clear definition of DNA, can be seen as fuzzy, as well as open-ended. We therefore considered KRAKE DNA to be an Opportunity Oriented Design [6] project, and as such we adopted the 1:10:100 approach [13]. The 1:10:100 approach uses traditional design phases, such as: research, specification, ideation, prototyping and evaluation, but it consists of three design cycles with an increasing time effort. The numbers in 1:10:100 suggest approximately the number of days one should take to go through a cycle.

During the 1-phase, you will have one day to deliver a design and prototype, the 10 phase takes 10 days and the 100 phase, about three months [5]. According to Van Turnhout et al. one can adapt the project phasing of 1:10:100 quite freely to ones needs: "In practice the actual number and length of iterations differs from project to project; the 1:10:100 ratio indicates planned upscaling of time and effort in three or more stages." [13]. Important to Van Turnhout's perception of 1:10:100 is the Quality Review Board (QRB). This QRB is an evaluation session, with (most of) the stakeholders, -led by a designer- that evaluates each time a new design proposition and sets a collective focus for the next iteration. When a QRB session is done in the right way, a lot of information has been revealed through and for the stakeholders, which lines them up (again).

2.1   1:10:100 Approach in KRAKE

In KRAKE the various project partners collaborated from different professional cultures, which brought an extra challenges to the project, because every partner tends to work preferably along work practices of its own profession. We, as designers, like to start a project with defining the goal and create a set of design guidelines that help us getting there. Due to the complexity of this specific project, and the ill-defined goal, the 1-phase with accompanying QRB session has been repeated for five times over the period of half a year. Each time new insights were discovered that sharpened the focus and created coherence in the project approach between the project partners. Initially this was a data-driven project, but during this phase we managed to shift to a focus on end users.

In the following 10-phase, the stakeholders were involved in the user centered design tools like cultural probes and co-creation to create engagement with the user's needs. In cooperation with the villagers the fundamental factors of success for a village became concrete, like for example, the organizing of a successful event or the need to share good ideas.

Finally, during the 100-phase, the product was developed on a detailed level in close cooperation with the project partners, working from the design guidelines as set during the first phases.

During the 1-phase, we used prototypes to define the goal and design guidelines. Each 1-phase with QRB session, a different prototype (design artefact) was delivered to make ideas tangible or to visualize the focus that had been set during the previous session. These prototypes fulfilled multiple roles, of which we see their function as boundary object [12] as the most important.

3   Boundary Objects

The term boundary objects was introduced in 1989 by Star and Giesemer, who described their findings about specific artifacts that serve as bridges between various cultures. According to Susan Leigh Star, boundary objects mediate between several (research) cultures, because of their 'interpretive flexibility'. The same object (that people can act toward and with) is flexible enough to be experienced and interpreted in different ways by different communities or persons, yet structured enough to maintain a common identity [11].

In addition, we use the study of Akkerman and Bakker [1], who look at the learning mechanisms that can take place at boundaries. Their study makes it explicit in what way boundary objects carry learning potentials and they reveal four mechanisms of learning (identification, coordination, reflection and transformation), in which we recognize reflection and transformation. Reflection enables the different cultures to look through each other's eyes and transformation can be found when the cultures 'clash' and recognize the shared problem space together. A new opportunity might arise from here [1].

The role of prototypes as a form of boundary objects in product development was explicitly studied by Carlile [3] and he defined their ability to 'represent, learn about, and transform knowledge to resolve the consequences that exist at a given boundary'. He mentions three characteristics that identify a boundary object as useful in joint problem solving. First, the boundary object facilitates a shared language for each to represent their knowledge. Second, the boundary object offers a concrete means that can be used to reflect upon strengths and weaknesses. And thirdly, the boundary object facilitates common ground to individuals, so that they can 'jointly transform their knowledge' [3].

Considering the theory about boundary objects, we review our project and recognize the 'representation, learning and transformation' [3] by prototypes in the project, as well as the learning mechanisms [4] reflection and transformation. We describe our case study based on these observations and learnings.

4   Case Study KRAKE DNA

When we -as a design team- entered the KRAKE project, the social scientists were struggling in the project due to privacy and cooperation difficulties that arose when collecting data in the villages. The team had to deal with two cultures who brought different views on the use of data. The idea to work towards a big data community was an idea from the scientists and wasn't supported by the community itself. Also the scientists were confronted with a 'boundary' between the German and Dutch culture around privacy and legislation, which made it difficult to create a coherent goal for the project.

This was the situation when the design team stepped in. We proposed to use the 1:10:100 approach [13], in which we planned to do five 1-phases (of one day each) spread out over approximately 6 months. Since the project was complex and ill-defined, the 1-phase was used to set a clear goal that every partner could relate to. Because of the many difficulties and diverging opinions it was necessary to apply multiple cycles of proposing a design prototype and reflecting on it. There was a lot to learn and hear from each other, before the focus became coherent.

At first, the social scientists were somewhat surprised and skeptical about our proposed approach to repeat the 1-phase five times. For them it felt unnatural to start 'designing' before they had a firm hold on the project and our proposal to 'redo' the design several times felt inefficient and wasteful.

However, this feeling quickly disappeared when it turned out that discussing the prototypes had benefits for the internal discussion about the DNA project among the social scientists and created new 'playground' to work with. Reflecting on the process we took interviews with the project partners and distinguished three main advantages of using a provotyping [8] approach such as in 1:10:100, matching the three characteristics of boundary objects that Carlile described [3].

4.1   Boundary Objects to Create Common Ground

Common ground plays a central role in almost any conversation [4]. Being able to discuss about concrete prototypes provides such common ground. The five 1-phases that were carried out, all consisted of a QRB session in which we presented a new prototype. This prototype fed the conversation and was discussed with social scientists of both sides of the border. Each paper prototype presents a design proposal, based on previous ideas and outcomes. And because the prototypes represent the DNA tool, it acted as shared reference point for the project partners to talk about. This caused cohesion and enabled them to talk and discuss starting on common ground. Even a plain prototype functions as a conversation piece by laying on the table as a tangible idea. As Koskinen et al., put it: "The props are simple, but they generate a genuine feeling of excitement when they are used" [9].

Before the 1-phase there was a boundary between the Dutch and German team and the designers. By using our ability to turn the research and ideas of the socials scientists into a prototype, we managed to create reference points that all project partners could relate to. Knowledge of the social scientists was combined with design skills and in this way a translation of both perspectives into a prototype created a common ground to build upon. It facilitated a joint focus that was strong enough to overcome difficulties that existed in the beginning of the project. At first, the discussion focused on the proposed product, but quickly shifted towards the underlying issues such as the purpose, vision and the goal of the project. In this way the design proposal as boundary object also created common ground for the project on a process level.

> "The 1:10:100 approach added value. [...] It provided structure and worked as professional counseling you could say." (Social scientist A)

4.2   Boundary Objects to Sharpen (Project) Focus

Secondly, prototypes forced the project partners to think beyond abstract ideas, because it is necessary to oversee concrete implications when discussing a project-outcome in a tangible form. This urged the project partners to explore their ideas and raise relevant questions about what they were doing. To enable this, the prototypes were designed for the purpose of conversation piece and as a means to reflect or provoke instead of functioning purely as a design proposal. This created a discussion that went beyond a product idea, but also sharpened the focus on a project and process level.

> "The 1:10:100 approach sharpened our focus. Several possibilities became clear and it strengthened us in what we were doing. [...] Also it became a necessity to communicate our message simple and explicit, because we saw the translation from the image in our head to the prototype that was shown. It appeared that we were not overthinking everything. The 1-phase showed us we needed a clear focus: what are we doing? For whom are we doing it?...the prototypes forced us to make choices and focus." (Social scientist B)

For example, during the first rounds of prototypes in the 1-phase, it was unclear where the project would head to. The goal was ill-defined and the general assumption was to use the data in the tool to create a database for the villagers. By creating prototypes relating to these ideas, the social scientists were urged to think about the true purpose and define the goal more focused. This led to a shifted focus from the data interest towards an interest in the users and creating a tool with added value for the villagers. It became a chance to highlight the entrepreneurship of the villagers and the valuable qualities and innovations in communities that truly formulated the fundamental factors of success for the sustainability of a village. Having a shared focus and common goal bridged all gaps between professions and cultures and created an acceleration in the process and helped defining a clear goal.

4.3 Boundary Objects as Window into the Future

Koskinen et al. suggests that design artefacts can operate as window into the future: "Design things are colorful, playful, and usually projective: they illustrate future possibilities" [9]. This is a third role the prototypes performed.

> "The five 1-phases were useful, because everyone showed new insights and discussed different functionalities. Potentials became clear." (Social scientist A)

The reflective value of being confronted with a design that is created out of vague ideas brings a lot of knowledge and communication on the radar of the project partners. When confronted with a prototype, the social scientist Shifted from a research towards a user perspective. Would it be accepted? Resonate? What would be the experience of the user?

'Taking another perspective is a way to begin to see things in a different light' [1]. When this knowledge is shared in a safe atmosphere [13], this enables everyone to communicate freely about the project and it allows to exchange ideas and knowledge, strengths and weaknesses in the process instead of through negative or personal discussions in the 'abstract'.

By experiencing a 'future design' it is possible to "spot problems and identify opportunities" in shared understanding [9].

> "The approach brought focus and raised new questions that we weren't aware of." (Social scientist A)

5 Discussion

This case study focusses on to what level design artifacts (prototypes) can function as boundary objects to structure a process and align project partners in working towards a clear goal.

The first challenge at the start of the project was the ill-defined character and the diversity in project partners involved with different professional and cultural backgrounds. The fuzzy process made it hard to proceed and to formulate a clear goal that was supported by all project partners.

Furthermore, the villagers – and end users of the DNA tool- were not willing to provide the scientists with data, because they were concerned with privacy issues. For the scientists, who proceed in the project by collecting data, this caused the process to get stuck.

The design approach in this project was 'the social act of drawing things together' [8]. Although the 1:10:100 approach of the designers was received with some hesitation, it soon proved its qualities. The five 1-phase sessions brought new insights to the project for all partners, because the design proposals that were shown as paper prototypes were reflective and created common ground to talk from. The prototypes bridged cultural and professional backgrounds, by showing a concrete proposal that was used as conversation piece. This led to a sharpened focus.

Furthermore the prototypes served as window to the future and created awareness for the needs of the users. With this insight the privacy issues that caused the research problems in the beginning, became irrelevant because the in-depth research of the social scientists shifted from data driven towards user centered; the user became the focus instead of the obstacle in the research. By triggering the users to share their successes and beliefs, concerns about privacy were replaced with proudness and willingness to share. The transformational process that took place as a learning mechanism [1] shifted the project focus towards an engaging community tool, that was supported by all project partners.

We found, when different cultures work together, prototypes can act as boundary objects and bridge cultural gaps by materializing and concretizing data in a way it is still open for interpretation, but also structured enough to provide a common identity [11].

For educators it might be interesting to introduce design methods into the world of social sciences to encourage cross-boundary working and learning. Turning data into valuable content is impossible without pushing boundaries and prototypes function as boundary objects that are perfect means to bridge gaps. This case study provides a good example of how to use boundary objects to do so and stresses the need for culture and discipline transcending projects and the need for a bridge to succeed a project. Design tools (such as prototypes) provide a good and useful basis for this.

The reflection made the project partners looking at the prototypes as users, which made the usability aspects and added value for the villagers much more obvious. In this way the project focus was sharpened further each iteration and whereby the assignment for a DNA tool initially was seen as a database, it finally became a useful instrument made by and for villagers to show their entrepreneurship with.

References

1. Akkerman, S.F., Bakker, A.: Boundary crossing and boundary objects. Rev. Educ. Res. **81**, 132–169 (2011)
2. Binder, T., DeMichelis, G., Ehn, P., Jacucci, G., Linde, P., Wagner, I.: Design Things. MIT Press, Cambridge (2011)
3. Carlile, P.R.: A pragmatic view of knowledge and boundaries: boundary objects in new product development. Organ. Sci. **13**(4), 442–445 (2002)
4. Clark, H.H.: Using Language. Cambridge University Press, Cambridge (1996)
5. Dorst, K.: Understanding Design. Gingko Press Inc., Berkeley (2007)
6. Emery, M., Flora, C.: Spiraling-up: mapping community transformation with community capitals framework. J. Community Dev. Soc. **37**(1), 19–35 (2006)
7. Hummels, C., Frens, J.: Designing for the unknown: a design process for the future generation of highly interactive systems and products. In: Proceedings Conference on EPDE (2008)
8. Johnson, M.P., Ballie, J., Thorup, T., Brooks, E.: Living on the edge: design artefacts as boundary objects (2017)

9. Koskinen, I., Zimmerman, J., Binder, T., Redström, J., Wensveen, S.: Design things: models, scenarios, prototypes. In: Design Research through Practice, from the Lab. Field and Showroom, pp. 125–144 (2011)
10. Mogensen, P.: Towards a provotyping approach in systems development. Scandinavian J. Inf. Syst. **4**(1), 31–53 (1992)
11. Star, S.L., Griesemer, J.R.: Institutional ecology, 'translations' and boundary objects: amateurs and professionals in Berkeley's Museum of Vertebrate Zoology1907–39. Soc. Stud. Sci. **19**(3), 387–420 (1989)
12. Star, S.L.: This is not a boundary object: reflections on the origin of a concept. Sci. Technol. Hum. Values **35**(5), 601–617 (2010)
13. Van Turnhout, K., Hoppenbrouwers, S., Jacobs, P., Jeurens, J., Smeenk, W., Bakker, R.: Requirements from the Void: Experiences with 1:10:100. In: Proceedings of CreaRE, Essen, Germany (2013)

Visual Quotes and Physical Activity Tracking: Can Aesthetic Pleasure Motivate Our Short-term Exercise Motivation?

Lígia Duro[1,2(✉)], Evangelos Karapanos[3], Pedro Campos[1], and Teresa Romão[2]

[1] Madeira Interactive Technologies Institute, Funchal, Portugal
ligiaduro@yahoo.com
[2] NOVA LINCS DI, Faculdade de Ciências e Tecnologia,
New University of Lisbon, Lisbon, Portugal
[3] Persuasive Technologies Lab, University of Technology, Limassol, Cyprus

Abstract. Empirical studies of activity tracking in HCI research have paid little attention to the impact of the visual presentation of motivational text messages on exercise motivation, even though, these days, motivational texts are often embedded in a visual presentation (such as visual quotes). Herein, we report the results of an online experiment with a total of 368 participants. Contrary to expectations, perceived aesthetic pleasure did not strengthen the motivating capability of perceived positive or neutral motivational text messages on the type of exercise motivation linked to the short-term (on the extrinsic-identified behavior regulation). Findings are discussed in the context of physical activity tracking services.

Keywords: Motivational text messages · Aesthetic pleasure · Exercise motivation

1 Introduction

In recent years, HCI researchers have questioned the feasibility of activity trackers as tools for creating behavioral changes [1–3]. One of the issues they have pointed out is the low impact of feedback strategies centered on displaying numerical measurements [1]. Individuals do not seem to perceive their past numerical data as meaningful [2, 4], and numerical feedback can actually have a detrimental effect on the type of motivation more predictive of long-term exercise adherence (intrinsic motivation) [1]. A possible alternative to showing numerical feedback would be to transform the quantitative data into personalized informative and motivational text messages.

In the short-term, motivational text messages can increase physical activity levels [5–7]. This likely happens due to their capacity to activate the extrinsic identified behavior regulation, which is linked to short-term exercise adoption [8, 9]. However, the HCI field has paid little attention to the current phenomenon of people sharing and accessing motivational text messages on image-sharing social media platforms, where these types of text messages are relatively and commonly embedded in a visual

C. Sylla and I. Iurgel (Eds.): TIE 2019, LNICST 307, pp. 109–118, 2020.
https://doi.org/10.1007/978-3-030-40180-1_12

presentation [10, 11] – designated commonly as visual quotes. For these people, motivational text messages may not only be about textual content, but also how the text is presented visually. In this paper, we describe the results of an experiment we conducted where the motivating levels of motivational text messages and the aesthetic pleasure levels of visual presentations were manipulated. We measured whether there was a difference in short-term exercise motivation when we perceived the visual presentations of positive or neutral motivational text messages as beautiful or ugly. Our results show that aesthetic pleasure levels did not influence the motivating capability of motivational text messages on the type of motivation linked to short-term exercise, contrary to our expectations. Implications of our findings are discussed within the context of physical activity tracking.

2 Background

2.1 Extrinsic Identified Behavior Regulation and Exercise Behavior

Self-determination theory (SDT) has been applied extensively to predicting and understanding health related-behaviors, including exercise adoption and exercise adherence among adults [8, 12]. In the context of this paper, the extrinsic identified behavior regulation that predicts exercise behavior in the short-term is considered next [8]. Identified behavior regulation is relatively self-determined and refers to behaviors that derive from the conscious valuing of an activity (the outcomes of the behavior are highly valued). An exerciser who volitionally participates in jogging gym sessions because it feels personally valuable to their health would be behaving for identified reasons [13]. By identifying with a behavior's value, individuals have more fully internalized its regulation (they have more fully accepted it as their own). However, the person's behavior is still extrinsically motivated because it is still instrumental (e.g., exercising to being healthy), rather than being guided by the activity's inherent interest [13, 14]. In sum, exercise outcomes are highly valued, and the behavior is performed with no pressure, but it is not particularly perceived as enjoyable in most cases. Studies have found that identified behavior regulation predicts better initial/short-term exercise adoption than intrinsic motivation [8].

2.2 Text Messages Interventions and Exercise Motivation

Several studies [9, 15] and systematic reviews [5, 6] have shown mobile text messaging interventions can promote physical activity among adults, with the majority of the studies being conducted over a period of 15 weeks or less [6]. Message content characteristics, such as gain versus loss frames [16], can influence the persuasive appeal of a message. Moreover, a recent early-stage work [9] suggests text messages can instigate autonomous motivation to do physical exercise, which in turn, is linked to positive behavioral exercise outcomes [8]. The study [9] which lasted one month and a half, found motivational text messages can instigate identified behavior regulation. In other words, the study found motivational text messages might help in promoting a conscious valuing of physical exercise. Nonetheless, more research is needed to examine whether the findings from this early-work are confirmed.

2.3 Visual Aesthetics in HCI

Tractinsky defined visual aesthetics as the beauty or pleasing appearance of things [17]. This hedonic quality, as instrumental qualities, contributes to a positive user experience with interactive systems. The HCI community's interest in the impact of visual aesthetics on the user experience started between 1995 with the findings of Kurosu and Kashimura [18] and 1997 with Tractinsky [19], both indicating that visual aesthetics influence the perception of usability of a system. However, several recent studies did not find a correlation between aesthetics and usability [20, 21].

Today, it is not yet clear how beauty impacts the overall impression of a product or influences other product attributes [22]. Nonetheless, there is a relative agreement in the HCI community that visual aesthetics can positively influence the user experience [21, 22]. Following Hassenzahl [22], one factor that can explain some of the inconsistencies found relative to the interplay between beauty and usability are the methodological differences in studying beauty. He distinguishes three general approaches: the normative, the judgmental, and the experiential.

The present paper focuses on the experiential approach. Experiential approaches focus on all-encompassing holistic experiences characterized by an individual's altered perception of their surroundings. They tend to preserve the complexity and richness of an aesthetic experience, in the sense that they do not look for ways to explain what specific characteristics of the object cause it to be perceived as beautiful or not. Rather, they are focused on how alterations in perception of beauty impact the assessment of artifacts.

3 Method

The primary research question of this study addressed the influence of perceived aesthetic pleasure on the motivating capability of motivational text messages on short-term exercise motivation. For this purpose, it was created a 3 * 3 factorial design where it was manipulated the perceived motivating levels of the text messages and the perceived aesthetic pleasure of the visual presentation. To try to achieve the three levels of motivation of the text messages—perceived motivating, neutral, and not-motivating—we started by creating a pre-study where 26 messages were assessed regarding their motivating capability. To try to achieve the three levels of the aesthetic pleasure—perceived beautiful, neutral, ugly—we started by creating a pre-study where 18 visual presentations were assessed regarding aesthetic pleasure. From the results of these two pre-studies, we then created the pool of visual quotes used in the main experiment. After the experiment was conducted the results were classified accordingly to the perception of how motivating were messages and perceived aesthetic pleasure. Next, we report the results of both pre-studies, and then we describe the main experiment.

3.1   Pre-study: Text Messages

A list of 26 text messages was collected from the Instagram account of the activity tracker Runkeeper [23]. We reviewed the posts from last to first until 26 generic text messages that do not refer to a brand or associated services were identified. Participants were recruited through Amazon Mechanical Turk [24]. Qualification requirements were defined: the number of HITs (tasks) approved greater than 500, and a HIT approval rate greater than or equal to 99%. Each individual was compensated with $.50. 100 individuals were recruited, but due to non-US nationalities, two individuals dropped out, which left 98 valid participants. Participants was asked to assess the 26 messages following a 7-item Likert scale, ranging from extremely motivating (1) to extremely demotivating (7), and the images were presented randomly, one at a time. After, participants were asked some questions related to their personal characterization (age, gender, nationality, education, exercise habits, and habits of seeing motivational text messages).

Results. The majority of the participants were women (71%), which might have led to gender bias. The sample's median age was 38 years (minimum = 20 years and maximum = 65 years or older). All participants have at least a high school education. Most of the participants reported exercising once in a while (42%), or never exercising (29%). Lastly, participants did not encounter motivational text messages related to physical exercise often. Only 6% of the participants reported encountering messages frequently. 31% of the participants reported seeing motivational text messages sometimes, 40% rarely, and 23% declared never encountering motivational messages. None of the messages were considered demotivating considering the mean of assessments. Therefore, we picked three messages assessed as neutral (*Did you get your dose today?* Mean = 4.3, Standard Deviation = 1.2; *How did you move today?* M = 4.0, SD = 1.0; *What do you run for?* M = 3.7, SD = 1.3), three messages assessed as slightly motivating (*Find your motivation.* M = 3.4, SD = 1.3; *Embrace the road in front of you.* M = 3.0, SD = 1.2; *Find your inspiration gear up and go.* M = 2.9, SD = 1.2), and three messages assessed a moderately motivating (*Let nothing stand in your way.* M = 2.4, SD = 1.2; *There's no feeling like exceeding your own expectations.* M = 2.2, SD = 1.0; *No matter what your goals are, the first step is to start.* M = 2.1, SD = 1.1).

3.2   Pre-study: Aesthetic Pleasure

To create variation regarding the aesthetic pleasure, author 1 started by creating several visual presentations and tested them with 6 to 11 participants. Following the results of these exploratory assessments, a pool of 18 visual presentations was selected to be assessed in the pre-study, which showed potential variety regarding aesthetic pleasure levels and would present relative agreement in the results among participants. In all visual presentations was used as text the anagram: *The quick brown fox jumps over the lazy dog.* A total of 195 individuals were recruited through Amazon Mechanical Turk and had received a compensation of $.50. Some individuals did not pass the criteria of having US nationality (n = 8), which left a total of 187 valid participants. Participants were asked to assess 6 randomly selected visual presentations. Visual presentations were presented one at a time. The aesthetic pleasure was measured by applying the validated scale Aesthetic Pleasure in Design [25]. Next, participants were asked to answer some demographic questions (age, gender, nationality, level of education). *Results.* The percentage of men and women participating in the study was relatively similar. 54% of the participants were men, and 46% were women. The sample's median age was 31 years (minimum = 19, maximum = +65). Almost half of the participants 42% reported having a bachelor's degree, and only two participants reported having less than a high school education. Each visual stimulus was assessed on average 62 times. Following the results of the aesthetic pleasure assessments, nine visual stimuli that varied regarding aesthetic pleasure levels were selected to be used in the pool of the main experiment. They were, the three visual stimuli assessed as the ugliest, three assessed as neutral, and the three assessed as more beautiful (assessed as slightly positive regarding aesthetic pleasure). Table 1 presents the means scores of aesthetic pleasure and standard deviations obtained for each of the visual stimuli selected, and Table 2 displays the correspondent visual presentations already with the text messages applied in the main experiment.

Table 1. Means and standard deviations of the aesthetic pleasure assessments of the visual stimuli selected to be used in the main experiment (scale values ranged from −3 [extremely ugly] to 3 [extremely beautiful]). The letter followed by a number corresponds to the visual presentation displayed in Table 2.

	Mean (Standard deviation)		
Ugly	A1 −1.93 (1.48)	B1 −1.89 (1.62)	C1 −0.90 (1.59)
Neutral	A2 0.06 (1.36)	B2 0.47 (1.31)	C2 0.48 (1.37)
Beautiful	A3 1.14 (1.17)	B3 1.19 (1.30)	C3 1.19 (1.27)

4   Main Experiment

The main goal of the experiment was to understand how perceived aesthetic pleasure influences the motivating capability of motivational text messages on identified behavior regulation. *Material.* A pool of nine visual quotes was created following the results of the two pre-studies described previously. Table 2 shows the pool of visual stimuli used in the main experiment. The visual presentations were displayed to participants in the size of 600*600 pixels. *Participants.* 400 participants were recruited through Amazon Mechanical Turk and were compensated with $.40. To participate in the study individuals had to pass some qualification requirements: location equal to the US, a number of HITs (tasks) approved greater than 500, and a HIT approval rate greater than or equal to 99%. The data obtained from participants were filtered by nationality and repetition of the IP address. Data from participants with nationality different from the US (n = 9) and data entries with a repeated IP address (n = 4) were removed, which left a total of 387 valid participants. *Procedure.* One of the visual stimuli picked randomly from the pool was presented to the participant. It was asked to the participant to assess this visual stimulus (visual quote) regarding aesthetic pleasure, using the validated scale Aesthetic Pleasure in Design [25], and its perception about how motivating or demotivating he/she found the text message presented in a 7-point item Likert scale. Next, it was measured the identified behavior regulation using the BREQ-3 scale [26], followed by some demographic questions.

Table 2. The pool of visual stimuli used in the experiment.

5 Results

60% of the participants were male, and 40% female. The sample's median age was 31 years (minimum = 18, maximum = 65), and all participants reported having at least a high school education. Most of the participants were regular exercisers. Only 21% of the participants reported exercising just once in a while, and 5% reported never exercising. Since we were interested in the effect of perception, participants were classified according to their assessment scores regarding aesthetic pleasure and motivational capability of textual messages (Table 3). As we can see in Table 3, only 19 participants classified messages as not being motivating. This result was expected because, during the pre-study of the text messages, not one of the messages were assessed as demotivating. Due to the small size of the groups within this level of messaging (Table 3, row demotivating), we decided not to conduct statistical analysis on these results and therefore discarded these results. A 2 × 3 factorial design was therefore obtained. The independent variables are: textual content perception with two conditions (motivating, and neutral), and aesthetic pleasure perception with three conditions (beautiful, neutral, and ugly).

Table 3. The number of participants within each condition.

		Aesthetic pleasure perception			
		Beautiful	Neutral	Ugly	Total
Textual content perception	Motivating	54	27	26	107
	Neutral	50	84	127	261
	Demotivating	2	4	13	19
	Total	106	115	166	387

To determine if there is an interaction effect between the perceived motivating capability of motivational text messages and the perceived aesthetic pleasure on the continuous variable identified behavior regulation, we ran a two-way ANOVA. However, due to the non-normal distribution we decided on separate Kruskal-Wallis tests. Two Kruskal-Wallis H tests were ran instead, however these tests did not allow for the interactions effects to be examined.

Two research questions were asked. RQ1: Does aesthetically appealing visual presentations influence the motivating capability of perceived motivating messages in identified behavior regulation? RQ2: Does aesthetically appealing visual presentations influence the motivating capability of perceived neutral messages in identified behavior regulation? To answer RQ1, we focused on group differences of aesthetic pleasure within the level of motivating text messages. The independent variable was the variable aesthetic pleasure that had three conditions: beautiful, neutral, and ugly. The dependent variable was the continuous variable identified behavior regulation measured using the BREQ-3 scale [26]. Due to the nature of the project being related to perception, we were not able to control how many participants would have each condition or group. The Beautiful group had 54 individuals, the Neutral group had 27 individuals, and the Ugly group 26 individuals for a total of 107 participants (Table 3, the row of the motivating messages). Data were not normally distributed in all cells. Therefore, a non-parametric test was performed to examine the group differences in identified behavior regulation. A Kruskal-Wallis H test was run to determine if there were differences in identified behavior regulation scores between the three groups of perception of aesthetic pleasure: the "Beautiful" (n = 54), "Neutral" (n = 27), and "Ugly" (n = 26). Distributions scores were somewhat similar for all groups, as assessed by visual inspection of a boxplot. Median identified behavior regulation scores (beautiful = 4.25, neutral = 3.75, ugly = 4.25) were not statistically significantly different between the groups, $\chi2(2) = 4.166$, p = .125.

To answer RQ2 we focused on group differences of aesthetic pleasure within the level of neutral text messages. The independent variable was the variable aesthetic pleasure that had three groups: beautiful, neutral, and ugly. The dependent variable was the continuous variable identified behavior regulation. The Beautiful group had 50 individuals, the Neutral group had 84 individuals, and the Ugly group 127 for a total of 261 participants (Table 3, the row of the neutral messages). Data were not normally distributed in all cells. Therefore, a non-parametric test was performed to examine the group differences in identified behavior regulation. A Kruskal-Wallis H test was run to determine if there were differences in identified behavior regulation scores between the three groups of perception of aesthetic pleasure. Distributions scores were similar for all groups, as assessed by visual inspection of a boxplot. Median identified behavior regulation scores (beautiful = 3.87, neutral = 3.50, ugly = 4.00) were not statistically significantly different between the groups, $\chi2(2) = 5.148$, p = .076.

6   Discussion and Limitations

Human-computer interaction literature is inconclusive regarding the impact of aesthetic pleasure (aesthetic appeal) in other factors related to user experience. While early studies found that visual aesthetics can impact the perception of the usability of interactive systems [18, 19, 27], more recent studies have questioned these findings and did not always find a correlation between aesthetics and usability [20, 21, 28]. In general, there is a relative agreement about visual aesthetics contributing positively to the overall experience with an interactive system. In this study, we were interested in exploring whether perceiving a visual presentation of a motivational text message as beautiful will strengthen the motivating capability of the message on short-term exercise motivation (in the extrinsic identified behavior regulation). Our results suggest that aesthetic pleasure does not influence the motivating capability of perceived motivating or neutral motivational text messages on identified behavior regulation. Following the literature, this does not necessarily mean that aesthetic pleasure cannot contribute to an overall positive feeling regarding the text message, but instead that aesthetic pleasure did not strengthen the motivating capability of the textual content in the type of exercise motivation linked to short-term exercise (extrinsic identified behavior regulation). For future studies, we suggest studying the interaction effects between the perceived motivating capability of the textual content and perceived aesthetic pleasure. One factor could interact with the other. In the context of activity tracking our findings mean that delivering motivational text messages as notifications (text-only) or as visual quotes (embedded in a visual presentation) can have the same impact in exercise motivation. We note, however, that we did not study the impact of using imagery in the visual presentations of motivational text messages. One of the limitations of our experiment was the amount of time we had to conduct the experiment. The experiment was conducted in a short time frame which may have affect the ability to capture the full effect of aesthetic pleasure. Future studies are needed to confirm these results. A second limitation of this study was due to their nature of studying perception. Since we did not know, although we had conducted pre-studies, how many individuals would assess the visual presentations as Beautiful, Ugly, or Neutral, we were not able to define from the beginning of the study the number of participants in each condition. This resulted in different group sizes. Finally, it can be argued that some visual presentations used did not differ much from each other. As such, the finding that perceived beauty does not have an impact could be caused by that. However, we highlight that our results are in line with another very recent similar study [29].

7 Conclusion

Nowadays it is quite common to encountering motivational text messages embedded in a visual presentation. This paper explored whether the aesthetic pleasure perceived from these visual presentations impact the motivating capability of motivational text messages on exercise motivation. Our experiment discovered that, opposite to what may be expected, aesthetic pleasure might not strengthen the motivating capability of perceived motivating and neutral text messages on exercise motivation. Research is needed to study the influence of the visual dimension of visual quotes on exercise motivation and engagement with physical activity tracking to help and understand how they can leverage healthy behavior changes.

Acknowledgments. This research was funded by ARDITI –Agência Regional para o Desenvolvimento da Investigação Tecnológica e Inovação, Madeira Island, Portugal, under the support of the Project M1420-09-5369-FSE-000001 – Ph.D. scholarship.

References

1. Etkin, J.: The hidden cost of personal quantification. J. Consum. Res. **42**, 967–984 (2016)
2. Lazar, A., Koehler, C., Tanenbaum, J., Nguyen, D.H.: Why we use and abandon smart devices. In: Proceedings of 2015 ACM International Joint Conference UbiComp 2015, pp. 635–646 (2015)
3. Kim, D., Lee, Y., Rho, S., Lim, Y.: Design opportunities in three stages of relationship development between users and self-tracking devices. In: Proceedings of the 2016 CHI Conference on Human Factors in Computing Systems - CHI 2016, pp. 699–703 (2016). https://doi.org/10.1145/2858036.2858148
4. Gouveia, R., Karapanos, E., Hassenzahl, M.: How do we engage with activity trackers?: A longitudinal study of Habito. In: Proceedings of the 2015 ACM International UbiComp, pp. 1305–1316 (2015)
5. Hall, A., Cole-Lewis, H., Bernhardt, J.M.: Mobile text messaging for health: a systematic review of reviews. SSRN (2015)
6. Buchholz, S.W., Wilbur, J., Ingram, D., Fogg, L.: Physical activity text messaging interventions in adults: a systematic review. World. Evid.-Bas. Nurs. **10**, 163–173 (2013)
7. Connelly, K., Mutsuddi, A.U.: Text messages for encouraging physical activity. In: PervasiveHealth, pp. 33–40 (2012). https://doi.org/10.4108/icst.pervasivehealth.2012.248715
8. Teixeira, P.J., Carraça, E.V., Markland, D., Silva, M.N., Ryan, R.M.: Exercise, physical activity, and self-determination theory: a systematic review. Int. J. Be. Nutr. Phys. Act. **9**, 78 (2012)
9. Tseng, Y.-C., Chang, H.-Y., Yen, S.-W.: The different effects of motivational messages and monetary incentives on fostering walking behavior. In: Extended Abstracts CHI Conference (2018)

10. Cocozza, P.: Read this and feel better – how inspirational guff invaded our lives (2014). https://www.theguardian.com/lifeandstyle/2014/nov/18/inspirational-quote-b(…)
11. Burnett, D.: Motivational posters: do they actually work? (2014). https://www.theguardian.com/science/brain-flapping/2014/nov/20/motivationa(…)
12. Rodgers, W.M., Hall, C.R., Duncan, L.R., Pearson, E., Milne, M.I.: Becoming a regular exerciser: examining change in behavioural regulations among exercise initiates (2010)
13. Standage, M., Ryan, R.M.: Self-determination theory and exercise motivation: facilitating self-regulatory processes to support and maintain health and well-being. In: Roberts, G.C., Treasure, D.C. (eds.) Advances in motivation in sport and exercise, 3rd edn, pp. 233–270. Human Kinetics Champaign, USA (2012)
14. Deci, E.L., Ryan, R.M.: The "what" and "why" of goal pursuits: of behavior human needs and the self-determination. Psychol. Inq. **11**, 227–268 (2000)
15. Toscos, T., Faber, A., Connelly, K., Upoma, A.M.: Encouraging physical activity in teens can technology help reduce barriers to physical activity in adolescent girls? Pervasive Computing Technologies for Healthcare 2008. PervasiveHealth 2008, pp. 218–221 (2008)
16. Latimer, A.E., Brawley, L.R., Bassett, R.L.: A systematic review of three approaches for constructing physical activity messages: what messages work and what improvements are needed? Int. J. Behav. Nutr. Phys. Act. **7**, 36 (2010). https://doi.org/10.1186/1479-5868-7-36
17. Tractinsky, N.: Visual aesthetics. https://www.interaction-design.org/literature/book/the-encyclopedia-of-human-computer-interaction-2nd-ed/visual-aesthetics
18. Kurosu, M., Kashimura, K., Creativity, O.F.: Apparent usability vs. inherent usability: experimental analysis on the determinants of the apparent usability. In: Proceedings of CHI (1995)
19. Tractinsky, N.: Aesthetics and apparent usability: empirically assessing cultural and methodological issues. In: Conference on Human Factors Computing Systems, pp. 115–122 (1997)
20. Hassenzahl, M.: The interplay of beauty, goodness, and usability in interactive products. Hum. Comput. Interact. **19**, 319–349 (2004). https://doi.org/10.1207/s15327051hci1904_2
21. Hamborg, K.-C., Hülsmann, J., Kaspar, K.: The interplay between usability and aesthetics: more evidence for the "what is usable is beautiful" notion (2014)
22. Hassenzahl, M.: Aesthetics in interactive products: correlates and consequences of beauty. In: Product Experience, pp. 287–302 (2008)
23. ASICS Runkeeper™: Instagram account. https://www.instagram.com/runkeeper/?hl=pt
24. Amazon.Com: Amazon Mechanical Turk page. https://www.mturk.com/
25. Blijlevens, J., Thurgood, C., Hekkert, P., Chen, L.-L., Leder, H., Whitfield, T.W.A.: The aesthetic pleasure in design scale: the development of a scale to measure aesthetic pleasure for designed artifacts. Psychol. Aesthetics, Creat. Arts **11**, 86–98 (2017)
26. Wilson, P.M., Rodgers, W.M., Loitz, C.C., Scime, G.: "It's who I am…really!" The importance of integrated regulation in exercise contexts. J. Biobehav. Res. **11**, 104 (2006)
27. Tractinsky, N., Katz, A.S., Ikar, D.: What is beautiful is usable. Interact. Comput. **13**, 127–145 (2000)
28. Van Schaik, P., Ling, J.: The role of context in perceptions of the aesthetics of web pages over time. Int. J. Hum. Comput. Stud. **67**, 79–89 (2009)
29. Duro, L., Romão, T., Karapanos, E., Campos, P., Campos, P.: How does the visual aesthetics of positively-framed messages impact their motivational capacity? In: Proceedings of the 31st European Conference on Cognitive Ergonomics. ACM (2019)

Raising the Odds of Success for Innovative Product by Experimentation and Utilizing Input of Future User

Georgy Laptev[(⊠)] and Dmitry Shaytan

Lomonosov Moscow State University, Moscow 119991, Russia
glaptev@econ.msu.ru

Abstract. A critical aspect of product development is inclusion of input from future users/customers. This input is invaluable for identification of innovative product features and functionality due to chaos, lack of predictability and structure that dominate at the first stage of innovative product development process, so-called Fuzzy Front End. This paper reviews the innovative product development challenges and aims to perceive how early-stage prototypes in combination with storytelling can help to better utilize user input and improve product management at the early stage of the process. We organized experiment-driven innovative product development process, immersed three cross-disciplinary product teams in design research and suggested them to experience through rapid prototyping. Guided by empirical exploratory study and statistical analysis we explore the accuracy of user input when it is provided based on different product representations (such as sketches, mock-ups and minimum feature set products) with and without storytelling.

Keywords: Innovative product development · Early-stage rapid prototyping · Storytelling

1 Introduction

In the era of "fast products" the process of new products development to meet customer expectations is becoming more challenging. A major reason of high failures rate of innovative products lies in misunderstanding who is user/customer/client and what they really need/want. In reality asking a customer about new product does not always result in the desired results, in particular when a radically new (breakthrough) product is being created [1]. Customers are not good in predicting what they really need/want and they are often not aware of potential solutions. Finding a different type of knowledge about user/customer "pains"/needs/wants can importantly contribute to product success. The critical questions here are how to avoid wasting effort by building a product that does not deliver value for users/customers and how to raise the odds of success of products that satisfy intended outcomes before running out of other types of resources.

This paper focuses on the collaborative exploration process for innovative product development (IPD). It evokes empathic resonance, co-creation and provides effective management of IPD process, which is of particular importance at the early and full of

C. Sylla and I. Iurgel (Eds.): TIE 2019, LNICST 307, pp. 119–128, 2020.
https://doi.org/10.1007/978-3-030-40180-1_13

uncertainty "getting started" stage. Collaborative design, as an effective approach at that stage of IPD, includes communication, sharing information and working together in order to find an optimal solution. We assume that the effectiveness of IPD, both in terms of productivity of communication within product team and outside of it while working with potential users/customers substantially depends on the form of representations of current results of IPD process.

The objective of this paper is to study and discuss different kinds of representations (design artifacts) of current results of product design in combination with storytelling at the early stage of IPD process. We aim to examine the way they help to effectively manage customer/product discovery and validation, based on inputs of future users/customers, inspire individual and collective insights for various participants of IPD process.

In the following sections we first set the ground for empirical studies, in particular, experiment-driven approaches based on human-centered design and customer/product development. Then, we provide empirical research and discuss representations of the different kinds of design artifacts together with storytelling. We conclude with formulation of the results and further research.

2 Experimentation and Representation within Fuzzy Front End of Innovative Product Development

2.1 Fuzzy Front End of Innovative Product Development

Innovative product life cycle includes invention, design, manufacturing, marketing, distribution, sale, product support and utilization. IPD process can be represented as three sequential stages (see Fig. 1):

- Stg.#1: Pre-development (early) stage, so-called Fuzzy Front End of Innovation (FFEoI), where a concept of the product and its feature set are determined and validated [2];
- Stg.#2: New Product Development and Validation (NPD&V) is a stage where a product are actually developed and validated [3];
- Stg.#3: Production and Market Launch (P&ML) is a stage of commercialization where a newly developed product is produced and brought to the market [3].

FFEoI is the most crucial stage of IPD process, since here product features and functionality are determined [4, 5]. In FFEoI product managers are responsible for managing both the complex process and the people in the product team with different background [6]. He is requires coping with multiple, often conflicting contingencies and finding balance between different approaches and behaviors [7, 8]. One way to manage activities within FFEoI effectively and efficiently is to apply exploratory style of management based on experimental learning with participation of the key stakeholders of IPD process. It requires utilization of future users/customers input. There are different ways in which users/customers can play an active role in IPD process. Given the importance of these circumstances, we discuss the managerial approaches in the following sections of this paper.

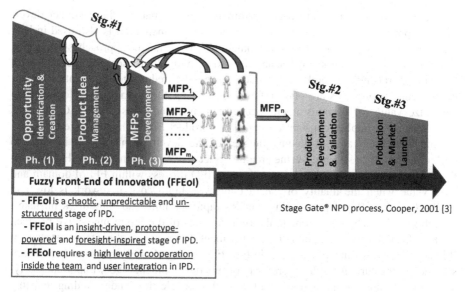

Fig. 1. Innovative product development (IPD) process.

2.2 Experiment-Driven Approaches with User/Customer Involvement

Experiment-driven approaches to IPD tend to focus on what to develop and are closely linked with customer development. Experiments involving users/customers are usually made to generate insights, getting feedback and to understand the relationship between specific actions, e.g. identification, creation and validation specific product features. Continuous experimentation is a basis of modern approaches/methods to create innovations. Among the most approved are human-centered design, customer development and lean product development.

Human-centered design (HCD) is a widely acknowledged creative problem solving approach which focuses on people and their needs/wants [9, 10]. HCD is a non-linear iterative process that begins with (1) definition of the problem and opportunity, followed by exploration of the user/customer and contexts of use, (2) generation of ideas through brainstorming, (3) building prototypes, (4) prototype testing, often carried out a number of times, and used of findings to refine the problem solution. Design thinking (DT) uses the designer's methods to match people's needs with what is technologically feasible, what a viable business can convert into user/customer value [11]. Participatory (so-called co-design) design is a form of HCD that actively involves users and others in all phases of a design process [12]. Users are not simply consulted at the beginning and invited to evaluate created product at the end. They are treated as partners throughout the process and become a part of IPD team as 'experts of their experiences'. In fact, the goal is to make IPD team and users work together, each contributing with strengths to clarify the problem and design task as well to explore design solutions. Participatory tools and techniques have a long-standing history in design studies and practice [13, 14].

Experimentation involving users/customers is a key part of the customer development approach [15, 16]. Similarly, continuous experimentation is also used in lean user experience and lean product development [17, 18]. Like the approaches mentioned earlier in this section, these approaches also strive to highlight user/customer centricity and aim at raising the odds of product success by reducing uncertainties. These experimental approaches are often referred to as "hypothesis-driven development" to maximize value for user/customer, reduce lead time and costs of IPD. Continuous experimentation implies constant testing of the product feature hypothesizes

and their user value as an integral part of the development process in order to evolve the products into high-value creation. Successive iterations of the "Hypothesis-Build-Measure-Learn" feedback loop structure IPD process within FFEoI domain and have value when the quality of the first guess is high, cost of rework is low and feedback is fast. Rapid prototyping enables rapid learning and minimizes mistakes. Thereby it raises chances to create the right features of the future innovative product.

For effective implementation of the experiment-driven approaches at the first stage of IPD process, i.e. within FFEoI domain (see Fig. 1, Stg.#1: FFEoI), continuous representation of the current results of product-concept development is very important. Early-stage prototyping is an activity and a tool valuable for understanding existing user/customer experiences and context, exploring and evaluating product design ideas, and communicating ideas/hypothesis within IPD team and to future users/customers [19].

2.3   Representation within Fuzzy Front End of Innovation by means of Early-Stage Prototypes and Storytelling

In FFEoI domain when many different ideas for a product are considered and accompanied by uncertainty prototyping focuses more on exploration [20, 21]. Early-stage prototyping, so called exploratory prototyping, is a tool to "get going" by building to think, helping a developer to uncover users/customers insights, generate and validate ideas, facilitate exploration of a design space [11]. Prototype is defined as a concrete representation of a part or a whole interactive system as an artefact, in particular, sketch, mock-up, CAD model, 3D print, simulation.

Early-stage/exploratory prototypes effectively serve within FFEoI domain of IPD process by aiding learning and communication. In the domain of learning prototypes often help to answer specific questions involving user interaction, for example, incorporating user feedback in a development process, assessing usability and definition of features and functionalities of future product together with users [19, 22]. Exploratory prototyping supports learning in two distinct ways: by framing design problems and exploration of various possibilities related to the product development, and by validation or verification of selected performance or functional aspects a product development [23]. Exploratory prototypes can also facilitate communication within FFEoI domain, both within the IPD team and with users/customers. They are one of the most effective tools to foster discussion to stimulate proactive thinking and a way to involve users/customers in participatory design [24, 25]. However, prototyping for rapid learning/communication is only feasible when artifacts are created quickly and inexpensively. Critical factors for progress within FFEoI domain are how fast the

IPD team is able to build prototypes, test prototypes and implement lessons learned in the next iteration.

In prototyping the contextual factors play a critical role in making decisions. By a context we mean surroundings and an entire setting or a situation. It is a risk to make decisions in IPD process without understanding and taking into account the context Storytelling can provide additional value to representation, in particular make it more realistic which assists to employment of user input [26]. A story comes into notice, provides clarity and inspires IPD team and stakeholders to act. There are many ways to communicate stories to our teams and stakeholders visually—storyboards, journey maps, empathy maps and scenarios of a user are just a few examples. Storytelling involves understanding of human motivations and emotions in order to truly move participants of collaborative activities. Stories build empathy and make the user needs and pain points memorable to IPPD team. Scenarios are descriptions users give by interacting with a product/system to achieve a goal under specified conditions and constraints. They provide information about a context in which a product has to operate in a user- and task-oriented way. Scenarios can be presented as rich narratives (e.g., day in the life of a user) or statements describing the triggers and a situation that encourages a user to interact with a product [27, 28].

In this study the different forms of storytelling are tested to improve learning and communication within FFEoI domain by better of representation in the beginning of IPD process by utilizing future user input.

2.4   Research Questions

Based on the literature review mentioned above, it is clear that representation by different forms of prototypes serves important purposes in IPD process of aiding learning and communication. To identify the benefits and impact of early-stage rapid prototyping within FFEoI domain of IPD process we organized co-creation design workshop to answer the following research question: How early-stage prototypes in combination with storytelling can help us to better utilize user input and improve management in FFEoI domain as well as to receive more valuable product concept?

This exploratory study is based on product design projects conducted by three teams in a framework of a 4-week co-creation design workshop. The workshop was organized for development of innovative product concept for fresh food delivery. The details of a design workshop, research method, data collection and analysis are presented in the following section.

3   Management of the Fuzzy Front End of Innovation by Utilizing Input of Future User

3.1   Co-creation Design Workshop "Innovative Product Design"

During a 4-week co-creation design workshop "Innovative Product Design", three cross-disciplinary IPD teams of six members were immersed into design research and "do it yourself". They gained experience in our rapid prototyping lab equipped with facilities (3D printers, milling and laser machines, materials, etc.) and materials for modeling and creative spaces in "d.school style" for team work. Design workshop can be described as a combination of "hard" (a set of equipment for rapid prototyping and creative space for team/project work) and "soft" (modern management methods and tools such as design thinking, customer development, lean product development) components for creating successful innovative products. Design workshop instructors and IPD team supervisors are both from the university staff and industry representatives from design, engineering and management.

The IPD teams had to carry their projects through all the steps of the creative problem-solving product design process within FFEoI, i.e. identification of customer/market/technology opportunities, development product ideas to meet customer demand and development of a product concept. The goal was to develop and validate product concepts, i.e. minimum feature set products (MFPs), for fresh food delivery. The IPD teams worked independently and iterated "Hypothesis-Build-Measure-Learn" feedback loop in 3 phases of FFEoI domain based on experimentation with users/customers (see Fig. 1). In the beginning, in the first phase (Ph.1) "Opportunity Identification & Creation", all three IPD teams were involved in the design research (user in-context interviews and observation) to gain in-depth understanding and empathy for future product user. Interviews and observations were conducted in the everyday user context which gave deep and reach view of thoughts, behaviors and life of user. The aim is to uncover "pains"/needs and find insights. IPD teams used design thinking tools, such as empathy mapping, trend mapping, knowledge capture template, knowledge wall, persona profile.

Effectively accumulated information allows IPD teams to move on to the next phase (Ph.2) "Product Idea Management", where they generate and select product ideas using creative techniques (see Fig. 1). At this phase, the first prototype appears in a form of sketch of the future product and its brief description. Concept sketches were forms of visual communication within and outside of IPD team and used to provide a specific and detailed view of a particular design idea. They called input, especially related to the product form. The following gives a summary of all heading levels.

Mock-ups were the next step of prototyping activities of IPD teams. They were created to evaluate the intended form/size and key elements of a product concept. Their construction assumes exactly the same look, feel, materials and other attributes as a future product will have. So they are not fully-functional but are the same in every other way.

In the third phase (Ph.3) called "MFPs Development" the IPD teams prototyped and tested a number of minimum feature set product (MFP). MFP is a "product" which has just enough features to gather validated learning about the product and its continued development [15]. Validated MFPs can go to the next stages (NPD&V and P&ML) of IPD process (see Fig. 1).

Therefore, the product representation within FFEoI domain was carried out by three types of prototypes (sketches, mock-ups and MFPs) for experimental learning and communication within the IPD teams and outside with the aim to utilize input of future users/customers.

3.2   Research Method, Data Collection and Analysis

This empirical exploratory study is based on quantitative analysis. A total of 192 potential users of the product for fresh food delivery were selected for evaluation three types of prototypes (sketches, mock-ups and MFPs). 180 of them performed evaluation. Each of three types of prototypes, sequentially created by each IPD team during the co-creation design workshop "Innovative Product Design", was evaluated independently by 10 users. In the same way each of three types of prototypes in combination with storytelling was also evaluated independently by other 10 users. The evaluation data was collected via the completion of the USE Questionnaire [29] which is successfully used by many companies around the world. The USE Questionnaire was constructed as five-point Likert rating scales. Users were asked to rate agreement with the statements on a scale from strongly disagree (1 point) to strongly agree (5 points). The USE Questionnaire itself is divided into four categories: Usefulness (8 questions), Ease of use (11 questions), Ease of learning (4 questions), and Satisfaction (7 questions). Statistical methods (mean, median, standard deviation, mean difference) were used in data analysis.

3.3   Results and Findings

The results of statistical analysis (mean, median, standard deviation, mean difference) of evaluation of three types of design artefacts, sequentially and independently created by IPD teams (#1, #2 and #3) during the co-creation design workshop "Innovative Product Design", are demonstrated in Figs. 2 and 3.

All three IPD teams with three types of design artifacts (sketches, mock-ups and MFPs) demonstrated higher values of means for the case of the presentation in combination "exploratory prototype+storytelling". Apparently, a better understanding of the product being created and context of using by potential users allows them to give more accurate and valuable feedback to the product developers. Therefore they have an opportunity to do the right iterations in the FFEoI domain to create the desired products more efficiently, i.e. faster and less expensive. The finding of the study shows that the efficiency of storytelling is higher at the beginning of FFEoI, i.e. combination "sketch +storytelling", and decreases at a later stage of exploratory prototype development ("MFP+storytelling").

IPD team#1	A.m.	Mean difference	IPD team#2	A.m.	Mean difference	IPD team#3	A.m.	Mean difference
Sketch	1,73	0,52	Sketch	1,89	0,83	Sketch	1,96	0,87
Sketch + Storytelling	2,24		Sketch + Storytelling	2,72		Sketch + Storytelling	2,82	
Mock-up	3,26	0,76	Mock-up	3,59	0,73	Mock-up	3,91	0,58
Mock-up + Storytelling	4,01		Mock-up + Storytelling	4,31		Mock-up + Storytelling	4,49	
MFP	4,27	0,17	MFP	4,28	0,24	MFP	4,53	0,18
MFP + Storytelling	4,44		MFP + Storytelling	4,52		MFP + Storytelling	4,70	

Fig. 2. Results of evaluation of the design artifacts created by IPD teams (#1, #2 and #3).

IPD team #1

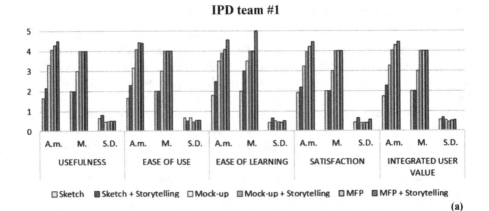

(a)

IPD team #2

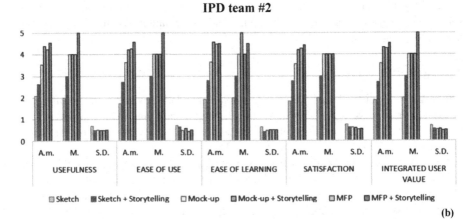

(b)

IPD team #3

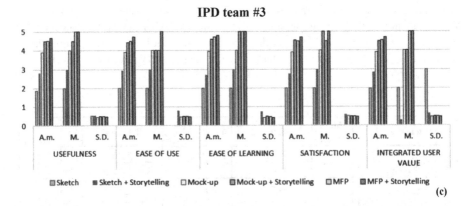

(c)

Fig. 3. Results of evaluation (usefulness, ease of use, ease of learning, satisfaction and integrated user value) of the design artifacts created by IPD teams (#1, #2 and #3). (A.m. - mean, M. - median, S.D. - standard deviation).

4 Conclusion

This paper presented results of exploratory study to identify the benefits and impact of early-stage rapid prototyping within fuzzy front end of innovative product development process. Experiment-driven approach involving users and exploratory rapid prototyping is a key part of in the early-stage of innovative product development process. We found that exploratory prototypes (sketches, mock-ups and MFPs) in combination with storytelling (storyboards, journey maps and scenario of use) can give great value for product developers within fuzzy front end of innovative product development process. A better understanding of the product being created and context of using by potential users allows them to give more accurate and valuable feedback to the product developers. Further work will continue to investigate different types of early-stage prototypes in combination with different ways to visually communicate stories and scenario of use to IPD teams and stakeholders, including digital format, to better utilize input of future users/customers.

References

1. Un, C.A., Cuervo-Cazurra, A., Asakawa, K.: R&D collaborations and product innovation. J. Prod. Innov. Manag. **27**(5), 673–689 (2010)
2. Kim, J., Wilemon, D.: Focusing the fuzzy front-end in new product development. R&D Manag. **32**(4), 269–279 (2002)
3. Cooper, R.: Winning at New Products: Accelerating the Process from Idea to Launch. Basic Books-Perseus, New York (2001)
4. Koen, P., Bertels, H., Kleinschmidt, E.: Managing the front end of innovation-part I. Res.-Technol. Manag. **57**(2), 34–44 (2014)
5. Pereira, A., Ferreira, J., Lopes, A.: Front end of innovation: an integrative literature review. J. Innov. Manag. **5**(1), 22–39 (2017)
6. Pons, D.: Project management for new product development. Project Manag. J. **39**(2), 82–97 (2008)
7. Lewis, M.W., Welsh, M.A., Dehler, G.E., Green, S.G.: Product development tensions: exploring contrasting styles of project management. Acad. Manag. J. **45**(3), 546–564 (2002)
8. Valle, S., Avella, L.: Cross-functionality and leadership of the new product development teams. Eur. J. Innov. Manag. **6**(1), 32–47 (2003)
9. Giacomin, J.: What is human centred design? Des. J. **17**(4), 606–623 (2014)
10. Brest, P., Roumani, N., Bade, J.: Problem Solving, Human-Centered Design, and Strategic Processes. Stanford PACS (2015)
11. Brown, T.: Change by Design: How Design Thinking Transforms Organizations and Inspires Innovation. Harper Collins, New York (2009)
12. Börjesson, S., Elmquist, M., Hooge, S.: The challenges of innovation capability building: learning from longitudinal studies of innovation efforts at Renault and Volvo cars. J. Eng. Technol. Manag. **31**, 120–140 (2014)
13. Brandt, E., Binder, T., Sanders, E.: Tools and techniques - ways to engage telling, making and enacting. In: Simonsen, J., Robertson, T. (eds.) International Handbook of Participatory Design, pp. 145–181. Routledge, Oxford (2013)
14. von Hippel, E.: Democratizing Innovation. MIT Press, Cambridge (2005)

15. Blank, S.: The Four Steps to the Epiphany: Successful Strategies for Products That Win. K&S Ranch (2013)
16. Alvarez, C.: Lean Customer Development: Building Products Your Customers Will Buy. O'Reilly Media, Sebastopol (2014)
17. León, H.C.M., Farris, J.A.: Lean product development research: current state and future directions. Eng. Manag. J. **23**(1), 29–51 (2011)
18. Hoppmann, J., Rebentisch, E., Dombrowski, U., Zahn, T.: A framework for organizing lean product development. Eng. Manag. J. **23**(1), 3–15 (2011)
19. Rosenthal, S.R., Capper, M.: Ethnographies in the front end: designing for enhanced customer experiences. J. Prod. Innov. Manag. **23**, 215–237 (2006)
20. Seidel, V.P., Fixson, S.K.: Adopting design thinking in novice multidisciplinary teams: the application and limits of design methods and reflexive practices. J. Prod. Innovat. Manag. **30**, 19–33 (2013)
21. Leifer, L.J., Steinert, M.: Dancing with ambiguity: causality behavior, design thinking, and triple-loop-learning. Inf. Knowl. Syst. Manag. **10**, 151–173 (2011)
22. Campbell, R., De Beer, D., Barnard, L., Booysen, G., Truscott, M., Cain, R., Burton, M., Gyi, D., Hague, R.: Design evolution through customer interaction with functional prototypes. J. Eng. Des. **18**, 617–635 (2007)
23. Elverum, C.W., Welo, T.: Leveraging prototypes to generate value in the concept-to-production process: a qualitative study of the automotive industry. Int. J. Prod. Res. **54**(10), 3006–3018 (2016)
24. Bogers, M., Horst, W.: Collaborative prototyping: cross-fertilization of knowledge in prototype-driven problem solving. J. Prod. Innov. Manag. **31**, 744–764 (2014)
25. Seidel, V.P., O'Mahony, S.: Managing the repertoire: stories, metaphors, prototypes, and concept coherence in product innovation. Organ. Sci. **25**, 691–712 (2014)
26. Dahlström, A.: Storytelling in Design: Principles and Tools for Defining, Designing, and Selling Multi-Device Design Products. O'Reilly Media (2019)
27. Hertzum, M.: Making use of scenarios: a field study of conceptual design. Int. J. Hum. Comput. Stud. **58**(2), 215–239 (2003)
28. Vincent, C.J., Blandford, A.: Usability standards meet scenario-based design: challenges and opportunities. J. Biomed. Inform. **53**, 243–250 (2015)
29. Lund, A.M.: Measuring usability with the USE questionnaire. Usability User Exp. **8**(2), 8 (2001). Management **27**, 377–392 (1997)

Author Index

Printed in the United States
By Bookmasters